1st EDITION

Perspectives on Diseases and Disorders

Influenza

Clay Farris Naff
Book Editor

PERSPECTIVES
On Diseases & Disorders

GALE
CENGAGE Learning

Detroit • New York • San Francisco • New Haven, Conn • Waterville, Maine • London

Christine Nasso, *Publisher*
Elizabeth Des Chenes, *Managing Editor*

© 2011 Greenhaven Press, a part of Gale, Cengage Learning

For more information, contact:
Greenhaven Press
27500 Drake Rd.
Farmington Hills, MI 48331-3535
Or you can visit our Internet site at gale.cengage.com

For product information and technology assistance, contact us at

Gale Customer Support, 1-800-877-4253
For permission to use material from this text or product, submit all requests online at www.cengage.com/permissions

Further permissions questions can be e-mailed to permissionrequest@cengage.com

Articles in Greenhaven Press anthologies are often edited for length to meet page requirements. In addition, original titles of these works are changed to clearly present the main thesis and to explicitly indicate the author's opinion. Every effort is made to ensure that Greenhaven Press accurately reflects the original intent of the authors. Every effort has been made to trace the owners of copyrighted material.

Cover image Margarita Borodina/Shutterstock.com

LIBRARY OF CONGRESS CATALOGING-IN-PUBLICATION DATA

Influenza / Clay Farris Naff, book editor.
   p. cm. -- (Perspectives on diseases and disorders)
  Includes bibliographical references and index.
  ISBN 978-0-7377-5253-3 (hardcover)
  1. Influenza--Juvenile literature. I. Naff, Clay Farris.
  RC150.I464 2011
  614.5'18--dc22

                                                  2010047522

Printed in the United States of America
1 2 3 4 5 6 7 15 14 13 12 11

CONTENTS

FOREWORD

"Medicine, to produce health, has to examine disease."
—Plutarch

Independent research on a health issue is often the first
step to complement discussions with a physician. But
locating accurate, well-organized, understandable medical information can be a challenge. A simple Internet search
on terms such as "cancer" or "diabetes," for example, returns an intimidating number of results. Sifting through the
results can be daunting, particularly when some of the information is inconsistent or even contradictory. The Greenhaven Press series Perspectives on Diseases and Disorders
offers a solution to the often overwhelming nature of researching diseases and disorders.

From the clinical to the personal, titles in the Perspectives on Diseases and Disorders series provide students and other researchers with authoritative, accessible
information in unique anthologies that include basic
information about the disease or disorder, controversial
aspects of diagnosis and treatment, and first-person accounts of those impacted by the disease. The result is a
well-rounded combination of primary and secondary
sources that, together, provide the reader with a better
understanding of the disease or disorder.

Each volume in Perspectives on Diseases and Disorders
explores a particular disease or disorder in detail. Material
for each volume is carefully selected from a wide range of
sources, including encyclopedias, journals, newspapers, non-
fiction books, speeches, government documents, pamphlets,
organization newsletters, and position papers. Articles in the
first chapter provide an authoritative, up-to-date over-
view that covers symptoms, causes and effects, treatments,

cures, and medical advances. The second chapter presents a substantial number of opposing viewpoints on controversial treatments and other current debates relating to the volume topic. The third chapter offers a variety of personal perspectives on the disease or disorder. Patients, doctors, caregivers, and loved ones represent just some of the voices found in this narrative chapter.

Each Perspectives on Diseases and Disorders volume also includes:

- An **annotated table of contents** that provides a brief summary of each article in the volume.
- An **introduction** specific to the volume topic.
- Full-color **charts and graphs** to illustrate key points, concepts, and theories.
- Full-color **photos** that show aspects of the disease or disorder and enhance textual material.
- **"Fast Facts"** that highlight pertinent additional statistics and surprising points.
- A **glossary** providing users with definitions of important terms.
- A **chronology** of important dates relating to the disease or disorder.
- An annotated list of **organizations to contact** for students and other readers seeking additional information.
- A **bibliography** of additional books and periodicals for further research.
- A detailed **subject index** that allows readers to quickly find the information they need.

Whether a student researching a disorder, a patient recently diagnosed with a disease, or an individual who simply wants to learn more about a particular disease or disorder, a reader who turns to Perspectives on Diseases and Disorders will find a wealth of information in each volume that offers not only basic information, but also vigorous debate from multiple perspectives.

INTRODUCTION

In early 2009 the world trembled in fear at the prospect of a global flu epidemic. The so-called swine flu, which erupted in Mexico, prompted calls for school closings and quarantines. The World Health Organization prepared for a pandemic. This seems hard to believe now, because the H1N1 flu passed without incident for most people. After the flu season ended and fears subsided, some charged that the whole episode was a hoax, drummed up by pharmaceutical companies to sell more vaccines.

To the family and friends of Judy Trunnell, however, the H1N1 epidemic was all too real. Complications brought on by the flu caused Trunnell, a thirty-three-year-old special education teacher, to die while giving birth. Pearl Guerrero, the principal of Travis Elementary School in Mercedes, Texas, said she still pictures Trunnell getting her first-grade students fired up with compliments and a captivating smile. "She was a young lady who had everything to live for," Guerrero said. "She was excited to have a new baby. She had so many things to look forward to and now she's gone."[1]

In succumbing to the swine flu, Trunnell became the first of more than two dozen pregnant women in America to die from the disease. Many of these women had previously been strong and healthy, but the strain of late-term pregnancy combined with the smothering effect of the flu on their lungs proved too much. In all, some six thousand Americans died of H1N1 infections, a number that was far lower than projections touted in the media yet a tragedy for each victim and his or her family.

This example in some ways typifies influenza. It is both routine and deadly. It sweeps through society every year without fail, and so people become casual about it. Many ignore warnings about prevention, and stockpiles of vaccine go unused. A 2002 study found that half the deaths from flu could have been prevented if everyone in the target population got vaccinated. Yet, most people pay little attention to the disease except for the occasional pandemic scare, when the media and authorities focus on it. Then, for a time, hysteria breaks out.

The fact is that flu is always a deadly threat to some and, once in an unpredictable while, a threat to many. In any event, having the flu is never pleasant. Influenza is a viral disease whose symptoms are somewhat like those of a bad cold, only much more severe. It attacks the respiratory tract. Symptoms include a runny nose, raw throat, cough, headache, fever, chills, muscle aches, and fatigue. While most people who come down with the flu survive it, annual deaths from the disease in the United States range from a low of three thousand to a high of forty nine thousand, according to the federal Centers for Disease Control and Prevention. Worldwide the average annual death toll tops out at about five hundred thousand victims. In some years, it is much worse.

The flu results from infection by one of various strains of influenza viruses. These are viruses that break into a cell and hijack its RNA, the chemical that carries messages from DNA in the nucleus to the cell's protein factories, called ribosomes. Instead of carrying out the DNA's commands, the ribosomes then begin to build copies of the virus. Eventually, the cell bursts, and all the copies escape into the victim's body, where they attack other cells. This process is subject to many errors, which makes the flu virus highly variable. Different viruses may attack the same individual and recombine inside the body, forming new strains.

This means the virus evolves so fast that scientists never know just what is coming. The flu virus's exceptionally swift evolution allows it to evade vaccines and jump species barriers. It also erodes public confidence in prediction and prevention. Occasionally, public health countermeasures aimed at the flu have gone badly wrong.

In 1976 army recruit David Lewis of Ashley Falls, Massachusetts, told his drill instructor at Fort Dix that he felt tired and weak. A day later he was dead. A postmortem determined that he had died of a fast-acting swine flu. This touched off fears in the government of a deadly epidemic. President Gerald Ford ordered a swift stockpiling of swine flu vaccines and appealed to the public for everyone to get vaccinated.

Unfortunately, several hundred vaccinated people suffered Guillain-Barré syndrome, a paralyzing and sometimes deadly neurological condition. Worse yet, since the epidemic never materialized, they need not have been vaccinated in the first place. Only a few other soldiers caught the flu, and they all recovered. The episode dashed many people's confidence in government scientists and the public policy their findings prompted.

This kind of error has led to widespread cynicism or indifference in the face of warnings. Even after warnings about the H1N1 flu saturated the media, less than a third of Americans got vaccinated against it. Among the high-risk, targeted population the rate of vaccination was just 37 percent. As events proved, the fears were overblown.

Sometimes, however, the warnings are justified. In 1918, at the close of World War I, an exceptionally deadly strain of flu swept the globe. Known as the Spanish flu, its timing was especially unfortunate because, as the war came to a close, millions of soldiers were moving from one country to another. This accelerated the movement of the infections, and soon the flu was everywhere. Unlike most flu strains, this one did not just pick off the weak and the elderly. It killed many strong young people as well.

Indeed, half the US soldiers who died in Europe fell victim not to the enemy but to the flu. By the time the pandemic had ended, at least 20 million people around

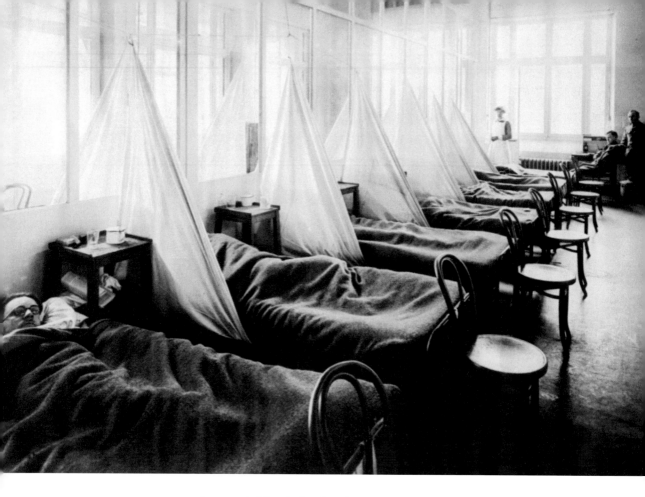

A hospital ward in France is filled with US Army soldiers infected with Spanish influenza. In 1918 the worldwide Spanish flu pandemic caused the death of nearly half of the American soldiers who served in Europe during World War I. (© Corbis)

the world had died. That number far exceeded the victims of the war itself. In the United States, an estimated 675,000 people died of the Spanish flu. It struck especially hard at people between the ages of fifteen and thirty-four.

Scientists fear that a strain of flu with similar virulence could return at any time. The constant churning of genes within the viruses makes such an event inevitable, many say. Researcher Robert Webster, chairman of the Virology and Molecular Biology Department at St. Jude Children's Research Hospital in Memphis, Tennessee, warns against complacency. "We may think we can relax and influenza is no longer a problem. I want to assure you that that is not the case," Webster says. Referring to the so-called bird flu, he adds, "H5N1 can kill 61 percent of humans infected, but it doesn't know how to spread from human to human. But don't trust it because it could acquire that capacity. So we must stay vigilant."[2]

Before that grim prospect can become a reality, scientists are racing to find new ways to combat the flu. Researchers at Mount Sinai School of Medicine have developed a vaccine that, in animal studies, works against multiple strains of flu. Others are trying to develop more effective treatments for those who come down with the disease. Still others are studying social networks to develop new strategies for containing outbreaks. Meanwhile, though, even if the feared pandemic does not eventuate, more tragedies like that of Judy Trunnell may be inevitable. The flu continues to kill.

Notes

1. Quoted in Associated Press, "Pregnant Mom Dies from Swine Flu, Baby OK," May 6, 2009. www.momlogic .com/2009/05/first_us_resident_dies_swine_flu.php.
2. Quoted in Min Lee, "Expert Warns of Complacency After Swine Flu Fizzle," *TriCity Herald* (Kennewick, WA), September 5, 2010. www.tri-cityherald.com/ 2010/09/05/1156860/expert-warns-of-complacency-after.html#ixzz0zh9Tq9EE.

CHAPTER 1

Understanding Influenza

An Overview of the Flu

Julia Barrett and Rebecca J. Frey

Influenza is among the oldest and most widespread diseases afflicting humanity. In the following selection Julia Barrett and Rebecca J. Frey describe the history, scope, symptoms, and treatment of this viral disease. Although most people who get the flu recover, it proves fatal, they write, in about 0.1 percent of cases. Fortunately, it can be prevented in many people by vaccination, although its ability to rapidly mutate makes targeting the disease tricky. Barrett is a science writer based in Madison, Wisconsin. Frey is a research associate at the East Rock Institute in New Haven, Connecticut.

Usually referred to as the flu or grippe, influenza is a highly infectious respiratory disease. The disease is caused by certain strains of the influenza virus. When the virus is inhaled, it attacks cells in the upper respiratory tract, causing typical flu symptoms such as fatigue, fever and chills, a hacking cough, and body aches. Influenza victims are also susceptible to potentially life-threatening secondary infections. Although the stomach or intestinal "flu" is commonly blamed for stomach upsets and diarrhea, the influenza virus rarely

Photo on facing page. A medical technician performs a test to analyze a flu virus by identifying its genome. (Health Protection Agency/Photo Researchers, Inc.)

SOURCE: Julia Barrett and Rebecca J. Frey, "Influenza," *The Gale Encyclopedia of Medicine* 3, 2006, pp. 2021–25. Reprinted by permission.

causes gastrointestinal symptoms. Such symptoms are most likely due to other organisms such as rotavirus, *Salmonella, Shigella*, or *Escherichia coli*.

The flu is considerably more debilitating than the common cold. Influenza outbreaks occur suddenly, and infection spreads rapidly. The annual death toll attributable to influenza and its complications averages 20,000 in the United States alone. In the 1918–1919 Spanish flu pandemic, the death toll reached a staggering 20–40 million worldwide. Approximately 500,000 of these fatalities occurred in America.

Influenza outbreaks occur on a regular basis. The most serious outbreaks are pandemics, which affect millions of people worldwide and last for several months. The 1918–1919 influenza outbreak serves as the primary example of an influenza pandemic. Pandemics also occurred in 1957 and 1968 with the Asian flu and Hong Kong flu, respectively. The Asian flu was responsible for 70,000 deaths in the United States, while the Hong Kong flu killed 34,000.

Epidemics are widespread regional outbreaks that occur every two to three years and affect 5–10% of the population. The Russian flu in the winter of 1977 is an example of an epidemic. A regional epidemic is shorter-lived than a pandemic, lasting only several weeks. Finally, there are smaller outbreaks each winter that are confined to specific locales.

Influenza Has Been Present Throughout History

The earliest existing descriptions of influenza were written nearly 2,500 years ago by the ancient Greek physician Hippocrates. Historically, influenza was ascribed to a number of different agents, including "bad air" and several different bacteria. In fact, its name comes from the Italian word for "influence," because people in eighteenth-century Europe thought that the disease was

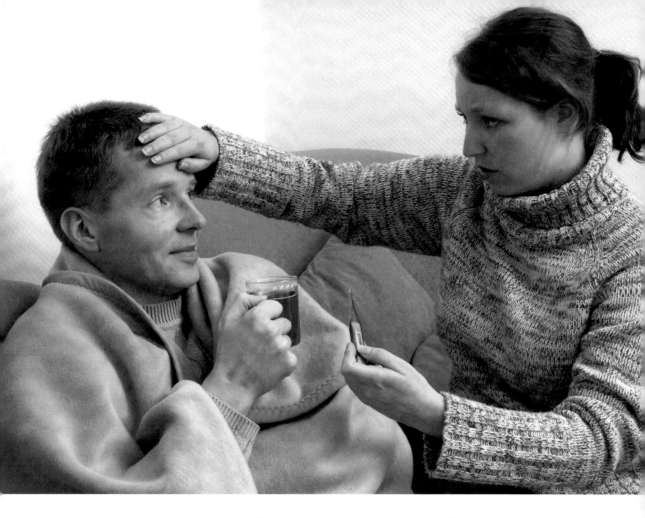

caused by the influence of bad weather. It was not until 1933 that the causative agent was identified as a virus.

There are three types of influenza viruses, identified as A, B, and C. Influenza A can infect a range of animal species, including humans, pigs, horses, and birds, but only humans are infected by types B and C. Influenza A is responsible for most flu cases, while infection with types B and C virus are less common and cause a milder illness.

In the United States, 90% of all deaths from influenza occur among persons older than 65. Flu-related deaths have increased substantially in the United States since the 1970s, largely because of the aging of the American population. In addition, elderly persons are vulnerable because they are often reluctant to be vaccinated against flu.

Influenza symptoms include headaches, dry cough, and chills followed by an overall achiness and a fever that may reach 104 degrees Fahrenheit. (© vario images GmbH & Co.KG/Alamy)

A new concern regarding influenza is the possibility that hostile groups or governments could use the virus as an agent of bioterrorism. A report published in early 2003 noted that Type A influenza virus has a high potential for use as such an agent because of the virulence of the Type A strain that broke out in Hong Kong in 1997 and the development of laboratory methods for generating large quantities of the virus. The report recommended the stockpiling of present antiviral drugs and speeding up the development of new ones.

Infection Causes a Rapid Onset of Symptoms

Approximately one to four days after infection with the influenza virus, the victim is hit with an array of symptoms. "Hit" is an appropriate term, because symptoms are sudden, harsh, and unmistakable. Typical influenza symptoms include the abrupt onset of a headache, dry cough, and chills, rapidly followed by overall achiness and a fever that may run as high as 104°F (40°C). As the fever subsides, nasal congestion and a sore throat become noticeable. Flu victims feel extremely tired and weak and may not return to their normal energy levels for several days or even a couple of weeks.

Influenza complications usually arise from bacterial infections of the lower respiratory tract. Signs of a secondary respiratory infection often appear just as the victim seems to be recovering. These signs include high fever, intense chills, chest pains associated with breathing, and a productive cough with thick yellowish green sputum. If these symptoms appear, medical treatment is necessary. Other secondary infections, such as sinus or ear infections, may also require medical intervention. Heart and lung problems, and other chronic diseases, can be aggravated by influenza, which is a particular concern with elderly patients.

With children and teenagers, it is advisable to be alert for symptoms of Reye's syndrome, a rare, but serious complication. Symptoms of Reye's syndrome are nausea and vomiting, and more seriously, neurological problems such as confusion or delirium. The syndrome has been associated with the use of aspirin to relieve flu symptoms.

Although there are specific tests to identify the flu virus strain from respiratory samples, doctors typically rely on a set of symptoms and the presence of influenza in the community for diagnosis. Specific tests are useful to

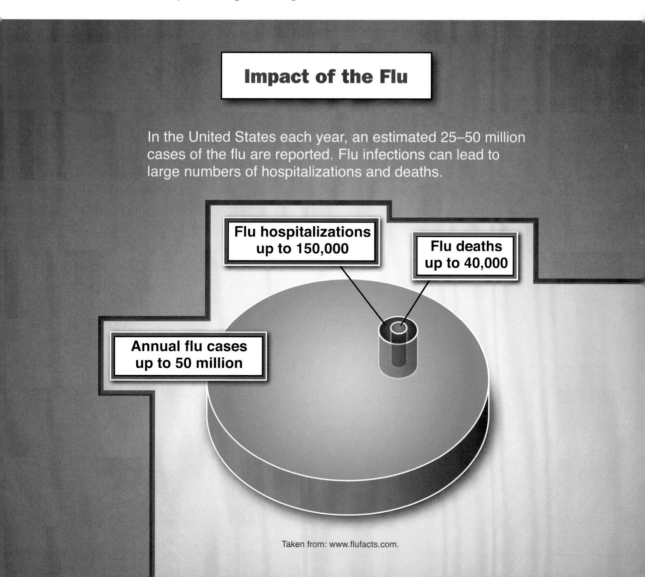

Impact of the Flu

In the United States each year, an estimated 25–50 million cases of the flu are reported. Flu infections can lead to large numbers of hospitalizations and deaths.

Flu hospitalizations up to 150,000

Flu deaths up to 40,000

Annual flu cases up to 50 million

Taken from: www.flufacts.com.

determine the type of flu in the community, but they do little for individual treatment. Doctors may administer tests, such as throat cultures, to identify secondary infections.

Since 1999, however, seven rapid diagnostic tests for flu have become commercially available. These tests appear to be especially useful in diagnosing flu in children, allowing doctors to make more accurate treatment decisions in less time.

Modes of Treatment

Essentially, a bout of influenza must be allowed to run its course. Symptoms can be relieved with bed rest and by keeping well hydrated. A steam vaporizer may make breathing easier, and pain relievers will take care of the aches and pain. Food may not seem very appetizing, but an effort should be made to consume nourishing food. Recovery should not be pushed too rapidly. Returning to normal activities too quickly invites a possible relapse or complications.

Since influenza is a viral infection, antibiotics are useless in treating it. However, antibiotics are frequently used to treat secondary infections.

Over-the-counter medications are used to treat flu symptoms, but it is not necessary to purchase a medication marketed specifically for flu symptoms. Any medication that is designed to relieve symptoms, such as pain and coughing, will provide some relief. Medications containing alcohol, however, should be avoided because of the dehydrating effects of alcohol. The best medicine for symptoms is simply an analgesic, such as aspirin, acetaminophen, or naproxen. Without a doctor's approval, aspirin is generally not recommended for people under 18 owing to its association with Reye's syndrome, a rare aspirin-associated complication seen in children recovering from the flu. To be on the safe side, children should receive acetaminophen or ibuprofen to treat their symptoms.

There are four antiviral drugs marketed for treating influenza as of 2003. To be effective, treatment should begin no later than two days after symptoms appear. Antivirals may be useful in treating patients who have weakened immune systems or who are at risk for developing serious complications. They include amantadine (Symmetrel, Symadine) and rimantadine (Flumandine), which work against Type A influenza, and zanamavir (Relenza) and oseltamavir phosphate (Tamiflu), which work against both Types A and B influenza. Amantadine and rimantadine can cause side effects such as nervousness, anxiety, lightheadedness, and nausea. Severe side effects include seizures, delirium, and hallucination, but are rare and are nearly always limited to people who have kidney problems, seizure disorders, or psychiatric disorders. The new drugs zanamavir and oseltamavir phosphate have few side effects but can cause dizziness, jitters, and insomnia. . . .

> **FAST FACT**
>
> According to eMedicine, the flu causes thirty-six thousand deaths a year on average in the United States alone.

Recovery and Prevention

Following proper treatment guidelines, healthy people under the age of 65 usually suffer no long-term consequences associated with flu infection. The elderly and the chronically ill are at greater risk for secondary infection and other complications, but they can also enjoy a complete recovery.

Most people recover fully from an influenza infection, but it should not be viewed complacently. Influenza is a serious disease, and approximately 1 in 1,000 cases proves fatal.

Prevention

The Centers for Disease Control and Prevention recommend that people get an influenza vaccine injection each year before flu season starts. In the United States, flu season typically runs from late December to early

March. Vaccines should be received two to six weeks prior to the onset of flu season to allow the body enough time to establish immunity. Adults only need one dose of the yearly vaccine, but children under nine years of age who have not previously been immunized should receive two doses with a month between each dose.

Each season's flu vaccine contains three virus strains that are the most likely to be encountered in the coming flu season. When there is a good match between the anticipated flu strains and the strains used in the vaccine, the vaccine is 70–90% effective in people under 65. Because immune response diminishes somewhat with age, people over 65 may not receive the same level of protection from the vaccine, but even if they do contract the flu, the vaccine diminishes the severity and helps prevent complications.

The virus strains used to make the vaccine are inactivated and will not cause the flu. In the past, flu symptoms were associated with vaccine preparations that were not as highly purified as modern vaccines, not to the virus itself. In 1976, there was a slightly increased risk of developing Guillain-Barré syndrome, a very rare disorder, associated with the swine flu vaccine. This association occurred only with the 1976 swine flu vaccine preparation and has never recurred. . . .

It should be noted that certain people should not receive an influenza vaccine. Infants six months and younger have immature immune systems and will not benefit from the vaccine. Since the vaccines are prepared using hen eggs, people who have severe allergies to eggs or other vaccine components should not receive the influenza vaccine. . . .

Certain groups are strongly advised to be vaccinated because they are at increased risk for influenza-related complications:

- All people 65 years and older
- Residents of nursing homes and chronic-care facilities, regardless of age

- Adults and children who have chronic heart or lung problems, such as asthma
- Adults and children who have chronic metabolic diseases, such as diabetes and renal dysfunction, as well as severe anemia or inherited hemoglobin disorders
- Children and teenagers who are on long-term aspirin therapy
- Women who will be in their second or third trimester during flu season or women who are nursing
- Anyone who is immunocompromised, including HIV-infected persons, cancer patients, organ transplant recipients, and patients receiving steroids, chemotherapy, or radiation therapy
- Anyone in contact with the above groups, such as teachers, care givers, healthcare personnel, and family members
- Travelers to foreign countries

A person need not be in one of the at-risk categories listed above, however, to receive a flu vaccination. Anyone who wants to forego the discomfort and inconvenience of an influenza attack may receive the vaccine.

A Survey of Flu Viruses

National Institute of Allergy and Infectious Diseases

Flu viruses come in several varieties. In the following selection the National Institute of Allergy and Infectious Diseases (NIAID) describes the major types and the classifications used to identify the viruses. The major types are called A, B, and C. Type A has numerous subtypes based on characteristics of the virus's surface proteins. NIAID is a federal agency that conducts and supports basic and applied research to better understand, treat, and ultimately prevent infectious, immunologic, and allergic diseases.

Influenza, or flu, is a respiratory infection caused by several flu viruses. Flu viruses are classified as types A, B, and C; type A has a number of subtypes. The flu is not the same as the common cold, nor is it related to what is commonly called the "stomach flu."

SOURCE: National Institute of Allergy and Infectious Diseases, "The Flu Types—Seasonal, Pandemic, Avian (Bird), Swine," NIAID, October 13, 2008. Reprinted by permission.

Seasonal Flu

Seasonal flu is the term used to refer to the flu outbreaks that occur yearly, mainly in the late fall and winter. It is estimated that between 5 and 20 percent of Americans come down with the flu every flu season.

Pandemic Flu

Pandemic flu refers to particularly virulent strains of flu that spread rapidly from person to person to create a world-wide epidemic (pandemic).

Avian or Bird Flu

In nature, the flu virus also occurs in wild aquatic birds such as ducks and shore birds. It does not normally spread from birds to humans. However, pigs can be infected by bird influenza (as well as by the form of influenza that affects humans) and can pass on the flu to humans. In 1997, it was discovered that a virulent bird influenza had skipped the pig step and had infected humans directly, causing a number of deaths in Asia.

These instances of bird flu in humans have raised concerns that if this type of flu could at some point be transmitted between people, a new pandemic would occur. Thus, the term bird flu or avian flu is currently being used to refer to a possible pandemic flu.

A Powerful and Common Disease

The flu, like the common cold, is a respiratory infection caused by viruses. But the flu differs in several ways from the common cold. For example, people with colds rarely get fevers or headaches or suffer from the extreme exhaustion that flu viruses cause. The most familiar aspect of the flu is the way it can "knock you off your feet" as it sweeps through entire communities.

The Centers for Disease Control and Prevention (CDC) estimates that 5 to 20 percent of Americans come down with the flu during each flu season, which typically lasts from November to March. Children are two to three times more likely than adults to get sick with the flu, and children frequently spread the virus to others. Although most people recover from the illness, CDC estimates that in the United States more than 200,000 people are hospitalized and about 36,000 people die from the flu and its complications every year.

Seasonal flu outbreaks usually begin suddenly and occur mainly in the late fall and winter. The disease spreads through communities, creating an epidemic. During the epidemic, the number of cases peaks in about 3 weeks and subsides after another 3 or 4 weeks. Half of the population of a community may be affected. Because schools are an excellent place for flu viruses to attack and spread, families with school-age children have more infections than other families, with an average of one-third of the family members infected each year.

Besides the rapid start of the outbreaks and the large numbers of people affected, the flu is an important disease because it can cause serious complications. Most people who get the flu get better within a week (although they may have a lingering cough and tire easily for a while longer). For elderly people, newborn babies, and people with certain chronic illnesses, however, the flu and its complications can be life-threatening.

The Virus and Its Types

A flu virus is roughly round, but it can also be elongated or irregularly shaped. Inside are eight segments of single-strand RNA containing the genetic instructions for making new copies of the virus. Flu's most striking feature is a layer of spikes projecting from its surface. There are two different types of spikes: one is the protein hemagglutinin (HA), which allows the virus to "stick" to a cell and initiate infection, the other is a protein called neuraminidase (NA), which enables newly formed viruses to exit the host cell.

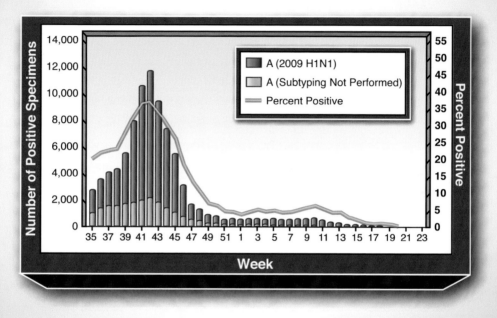

H1N1-Positive Flu Tests Peaked in Mid-October 2009

Legend:
- A (2009 H1N1)
- A (Subtyping Not Performed)
- Percent Positive

Y-axis (left): Number of Positive Specimens — 0, 2,000, 4,000, 6,000, 8,000, 10,000, 12,000, 14,000

Y-axis (right): Percent Positive — 0, 5, 10, 15, 20, 25, 30, 35, 40, 45, 50, 55

X-axis: Week — 35, 37, 39, 41, 43, 45, 47, 49, 51, 1, 3, 5, 7, 9, 11, 13, 15, 17, 19, 21, 23

Taken from: Centers for Disease Control and Prevention Flu View, "2009–2010 Influenza Season Week 20 Ending May 22, 2010," May 2010. www.cdc.gov/flu/weekly.

Influenza viruses are classified as type A, B, or C based upon their protein composition. Type A viruses are found in many kinds of animals, including ducks, chickens, pigs, and whales, and also humans. The type B virus widely circulates in humans. Type C has been found in humans, pigs, and dogs and causes mild respiratory infections, but does not spark epidemics.

Type A influenza is the most frightening of the three. It is believed responsible for the global outbreaks of 1918, 1957, and 1968. Type A viruses are subdivided into groups based on two surface proteins, HA and NA. Scientists have characterized 16 HA subtypes and 9 NA subtypes.

Type A subtypes are classified by a naming system that includes the place the strain was first found, a lab identification number, the year of discovery, and, in parentheses, the type of HA and NA it possesses, for example, A/Hong Kong/156/97 (H5N1). If the virus infects non-humans, the host species is included before the geographical site, as in A/Chicken/Hong Kong/G9/97 (H9N2). There are no type B or C subtypes.

Jumping Species Barriers

In nature, the flu virus is found in wild aquatic birds such as ducks and shore birds. It has persisted in these birds for millions of years and does not typically harm them. But the frequently mutating flu viruses can readily jump the species barrier from wild birds to domesticated ducks and then to chickens. From there, the next stop in the infectious chain is often pigs.

> **FAST FACT**
>
> In contrast to the type A flu viruses, type B flu is found only in humans.

Pigs can be infected by both bird (avian) influenza and the form of influenza that infects humans. In a setting such as a farm where chickens, humans, and pigs live in close proximity, pigs act as an influenza virus mixing bowl. If a pig is infected with avian and human flu simultaneously, the two types of virus may exchange genes. Such a "reassorted" flu virus can sometimes spread from pigs to people.

Depending on the precise assortment of bird-type flu proteins that make it into the human population, the flu may be more or less severe.

In 1997, for the first time, scientists found that bird influenza skipped the pig step and infected humans directly. Alarmed health officials feared a worldwide epidemic (a pandemic). But, fortunately, the virus could not pass between people and thus did not spark an epidemic. Scientists speculate that chickens may now also have the receptor used by human-type viruses.

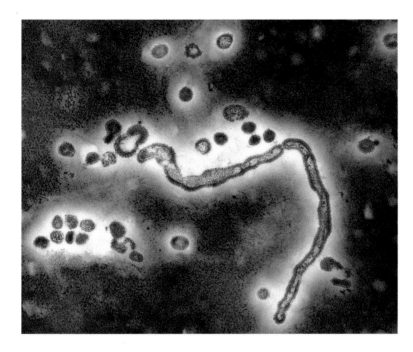

A colored transmission electron micrograph shows the influenza A virus, the most deadly of the three influenza virus types. (Hazel Appleton, Health Protection Agency Centre for Infections/Photo Researchers, Inc.)

Constant Genetic Changes

Influenza virus is one of the most changeable of viruses. These genetic changes may be small and continuous or large and abrupt.

Small, continuous changes happen in type A and type B influenza as the virus makes copies of itself. The process is called antigenic drift. The drifting is frequent enough to make the new strain of virus often unrecognizable to the human immune system. For this reason, a new flu vaccine must be produced each year to combat that year's prevalent strains.

Type A influenza also undergoes infrequent and sudden changes, called antigenic shift. Antigenic shift occurs when two different flu strains infect the same cell and exchange genetic material. The novel assortment of HA or NA proteins in a shifted virus creates a new influenza A subtype. Because people have little or no immunity to such a new subtype, their appearance tends to coincide with a very severe flu epidemic or pandemic.

Flu Viruses Are Difficult to Predict and Contain

Marc Siegel

In the following selection physician Marc Siegel describes and compares two flu outbreaks. Starting with the most deadly, the 1918 flu pandemic, Siegel describes how a flu virus sickened and killed at least 50 million people. He then explains how public health officials, reacting to an outbreak of swine flu in 1976 and recalling the severity of the 1918 outbreak, made policy mistakes that ended up harming some people and costing the public millions for a pandemic that never materialized. Siegel illustrates how hard it is to forecast the disease and its effects and how difficult it is to get the public policy response right.

A s even the most casual bird flu followers must know by now, back in 1918 an influenza virus killed—by many estimates—more than 50 million people. . . .

In the fall of 1918, around the globe, perhaps beginning in the Indian army, perhaps beginning in the American

SOURCE: Marc Siegel, "Chapter 3: Spanish Flu Versus Swine Flu," *Bird Flu: Everything You Need to Know About the Next Pandemic,* John Wiley & Sons, 2006, pp. 55, 58–67. Reproduced with permission of John Wiley & Sons, Inc.

army, an infection took hold that was at first perceived to be no more than a cold. However, as it spread from America through Europe, it became more deadly. It quickly killed many who lived in the poor conditions of the combat trenches, but far more than that, it sped around the globe, killing tens of millions of people, including an estimated 17 million in India, where it did most of its damage.

But few countries were spared. Surprisingly, the flu was most deadly for young adults, between the ages of twenty and forty, rather than the very young and the elderly, whom most flus affect. Some experts have postulated in retrospect that it was the heightened immune response that healthy people can muster that somehow did them in. Their lungs may have filled up with infection-fighting secretions they couldn't clear. Most experts agree that the most common cause of death was pneumonia and respiratory failure. Most likely, the pneumonia was due to a secondary bacterial pneumonia for which there were no antibiotic treatments available at the time. For those who survived, the virus also appears to have caused neurological side effects in many patients, including an inflammation of the brain (encephalopathy), which often led to permanent disabilities.

Deadlier than War

The flu also brought out many other chronic conditions such as heart disease, asthma, and diabetes, for which there were no ready treatments.

In the end, the Spanish flu infected at least 28 percent of all Americans, and at least 675,000 died, ten times as many as in the Great War [World War I]. Half of the American soldiers who died in Europe died from influenza rather than from combat.

As noted in the *Journal of the American Medical Association*'s final edition of 1918:

> 1918 has gone: a year momentous as the termination of the most cruel war in the annals of the human race; a year which marked the end, at least for a time, of man's

destruction of man; unfortunately a year in which developed a most fatal infectious disease causing the death of hundreds of thousands of human beings. Medical science for four and one-half years devoted itself to putting men on the firing line and keeping them there. Now it must turn with its whole might to combating the greatest enemy of all: infectious disease.

Even with the Spanish flu, the worst of all plagues, most victims recovered, and their experience generally was a more intense version of the expected weeklong course of fever, aches, chills, and nausea that characterized all influenza. But a substantial minority endured much worse. They were exhausted, with earaches, headaches, high fever, and difficult breathing.

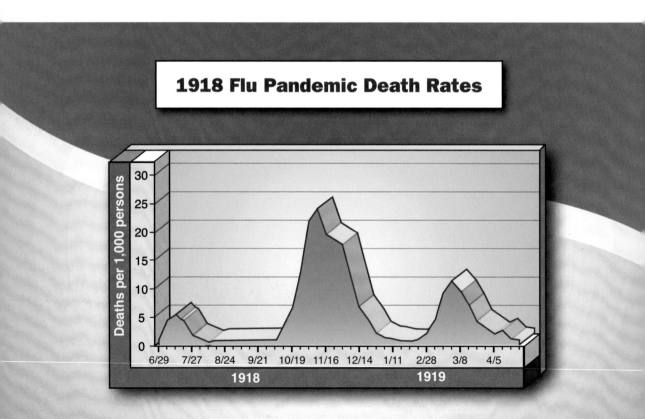

Taken from: J.K. Taubenberger and D.M. Morens, "1918 Influenza: the Mother of All Pandemics," January 2006. www.cdc.gov/ncidod/EID/vol12no01/05-0979.htm.

Doctors with little experience diagnosing viruses (they still didn't really know what a virus was) often confused the Spanish flu with a cold until the patients were very sick.

The Blue Death

Some patients died rapidly, sometimes overnight. They turned cyanotic (meaning they turned blue), struggled for air, and were choked by their blood-tinged secretions. As the disease progressed and pneumonia set in, they began to bleed profusely—from the nose, the ears, and the mouth. Some still recovered. But if cyanosis appeared, physicians treated patients as terminal. Autopsies would show a disease that ravaged almost every internal organ.

The pandemic circled the globe, often following trade routes and shipping lines. Outbreaks coursed through North America, Europe, Asia, Brazil, and the South Pacific. Soldiers spread it to far lands on ships. . . .

Entire Navy fleets were sick with the disease and were too ill to fight, and military hospitals, already overcome with the war wounded (including burns from mustard gas), were unequipped to treat the flu. Soldiers lived and traveled in cramped conditions conducive to the spread of the virus.

Inadequate Medical Response

On top of this, there was a shortage of physicians and nurses. Medical personnel discovered that having potentially infected people wear a surgical mask helped limit the spread of infection—until they ran out of gauze to make surgical masks. They understood that administering oxygen to patients in distress was helpful, but they didn't have the means to administer it to even a small percentage of the patients who needed it. They understood that overcrowding soldiers into barracks and packing patients wall to wall in hospitals were making things worse, but they had no alternative. The differences between the resources

Female clerks wear surgical masks to protect against the influenza virus in 1918. The measure succeeded only in slowing the spread of the virus. (© Bettmann/Corbis)

available to us today and those available a century ago are staggering.

The nation even experienced a shortage of coffins and grave diggers. Funerals were limited to fifteen minutes. Bodies piled up, as they had during the bubonic plague of the fourteenth century, in hospitals, in carts, in homes, in hallways, in the streets.

The Red Cross responded to the nursing shortage by asking for volunteers and by creating the National Committee on Influenza. Emergency hospitals were created to take in those sick with influenza as well as those arriving sick from overseas. With one quarter of the United States and one fifth of the world infected, it was impossible to escape from it, though the wealthy and the famous were fairly successful at sequestering themselves. But even President Woodrow Wilson caught influenza in early 1919, while negotiating the Treaty of Versailles.

Scientists, using the recently accepted germ theory, worked unsuccessfully on a vaccine. Public health officials, capitalizing on restrictions already in place for the war, tried to restrict movements between U.S. cities. Railroads wouldn't accept passengers without signed documentation attesting to no infection. But overall, the public health response was characterized by confusion, disorganization, ineffectiveness, and edicts that weren't followed.

The Pandemic Ends

And then, as quickly as it had come, in 1919, perhaps aided by the coming of spring, when flu viruses traditionally fail to thrive, the Spanish flu died out.

After 1918, research identified the virus that causes influenza as well as the bacteria-like pneumonia that causes its secondary, life-threatening complications. Public health officials are far better these days than in 1918 at public education and promoting public co-operation. One can only speculate about what would have happened in 1918 if they had available to them even a tenth of the technology and methods that we have today.

Still, the world is much more densely populated, and air travel allows people to travel (and potentially spread disease) to far-off places in only a matter of hours. But while a plane covers a lot ground very quickly, a 1918 military ship in the middle of the high seas, densely packed with exhausted young men eating and sleeping in close quarters, makes for a better environment to grow and spread a virus.

As hard as it is to make direct comparisons between 1918 and the present, it's easier to make comparisons with the swine flu, which occurred just thirty years ago.

Swine Flu Appears

On February 5, 1976, nineteen-year-old Private David Lewis of Massachusetts told his drill instructor at Fort Dix that he felt tired and weak. Nevertheless, he participated in a training hike and within twenty-four hours he was dead. Two weeks after his death, health officials, calling Lewis the "index case" and having isolated five hundred other cases of what they called "swine flu" in other recruits who hadn't gotten sick and four who had, disclosed to the American public that there was concern about a possible epidemic. Public panic ensued, as health officials reasoned that any flu that was able to reach so many people so fast was capable of becoming a worldwide plague.

With the specter of 1918 firmly in their minds, public health officials quickly considered the possibility of mass inoculations before the next flu season, worrying that as in 1918 the flu virus might get stronger by its second season, or "wave." . . .

Back in 1976, operating on the assumption that the swine flu virus that had been discovered was very similar to the 1918 flu bug, public health officials, leaders, and subsequently the public were all worried. No one knew how the swine flu had gotten to Fort Dix, but all were concerned that it could spread rapidly from there.

Weeks after Private Lewis died, doctors from the Centers for Disease Control, including the director, Dr. David Spencer, the sagacious polio vaccine inventors [Jonas] Salk and [Albert] Sabin, and other officials met in Washington, D.C., to decide what to do. They were concerned about swine flu, but they were also concerned that attempts to rapidly immunize the public would interrupt work on many other diseases. They could only imagine, however, the complaints doctors would face if an epidemic broke out and vaccines weren't ready. At the same time, they couldn't help wondering what would happen if everyone was inoculated for a plague that didn't happen.

By March 1976, Dr. Spencer had lined up most of the medical establishment behind his plan to ask the president for $135 million to mass vaccinate the country.

Politics Played a Role

But there may have been more to it than simple medical concerns. It may also have been political. In his book *Pure Politics and Impure Science*, Arthur M. Silverstein suggests that presidential politics played a heavy role in this decision, as President Gerald Ford, up for re-election and under the influence of America's big drug manufacturers, wanted to be seen as a hero.

On March 24, the day after a surprise loss to Ronald Reagan in the North Carolina Republican primary, Ford made his announcement to the public and prepared to take this battle to Congress. Meanwhile, the drug makers were insisting that the government take liability for any harmful side effects from a hastily made vaccine. Congressional hearings stretched on into the early summer, with some doubting Thomases (I'm not the first doctor, clearly, to have doubts) pointing out that swine flu hadn't extended beyond Fort Dix in its "first wave."

> **FAST FACT**
>
> Influenza viruses mutate rapidly because they use their host cell's RNA rather than its DNA to replicate. RNA is less stable and therefore subject to more copying errors, resulting in mutations.

Ultimately, the president and his experts prevailed, and on August 12, 1976, Congress approved the funding. Dr. W. Delano Meriwether of the Department of Health, Education and Welfare, a thirty-three-year-old physician and world-class sprinter, was put in charge of the project and given until the end of the year to inoculate all 220 million Americans against swine flu.

When insurance companies refused to provide coverage to the vaccine manufacturers, the government finally agreed to accept liability for claims of adverse events. This obstacle having been cleared, the National Influenza Immunization Program (NIIP) officially started in October 1976.

Deadly Reactions to the Vaccine

By October 1 the serum was ready, and the public health system had organized doctors, nurses, and paraprofessionals to give out the shots. But within days, several people who had taken the shot fell seriously ill. Three elderly people in Pennsylvania had their shots and died just a few hours later of heart attacks, which caused the program to be immediately suspended in that state.

Other states pressed on, even as more reports of adverse side effects came out.

The number of vaccinations given each week increased rapidly from less than 1 million in early October to more than 4 million in the later weeks of the month, and reached a peak of more than 6 million doses a week by the middle of November 1976. The NIIP was unique in the annals of epidemiology: an organized surveillance effort was in place from the very beginning, and over 40 million people were vaccinated during the short time the NIIP was in effect. However, on December 16, 1976, the NIIP was suspended following reports from more than ten states of Guillain-Barré syndrome (GBS) in vaccinees. By January 1977, more than five hundred cases of GBS had been reported, with twenty-five deaths. The government suspended the program. Millions of dollars in lawsuits followed.

Erring on the Side of Caution

One question you regularly hear in the media is, could we react to a pandemic if we needed to? In 1976, our public health officials pulled off an astonishing public health feat to counter what they thought was an emerging plague based on 1918 fears. But, rather than learn from this event now, we leave it buried in history. Public health officials both then and now speak with an apparent certainty that does not always reflect the amount of speculation involved. Swine flu showed not only that you can rush to judgment, wasting time and money ramping up for a worst-case scenario that never comes, but that in doing so, there may also be significant costs to people's health.

The swine flu scare helped foster cynicism and distrust of federal policy makers and health officials. But Joseph Califano, who subsequently became secretary of the Department of Health, Education and Welfare under President [Jimmy] Carter, continued to maintain that doctors had had no choice but to err on the side of caution, and should do so again if faced with the threat of another killer plague with the potential to kill millions.

A Faster, More Effective Test to Diagnose Flu

Katie Walter

Flu moves fast. The speed of transmission has put pressure on researchers to develop faster methods of diagnosis. In the following selection Katie Walter reports on hopeful developments at the Lawrence Livermore National Laboratory in Livermore, California. Scientists there are working to develop methods that not only diagnose a flu infection more quickly but also identify the exact type of virus that causes it. Called the "FluID$_X$" system, the testing device can diagnose other respiratory viruses in addition to the flu, according to Walter. By decreasing the time in which test results are available, she reports, FluID$_X$ allows patients to begin receiving treatment more quickly than earlier diagnostic tests allowed. Walter is a science writer based at the Lawrence Livermore National Laboratory.

People with flulike symptoms who seek treatment at a medical clinic or hospital often must wait several hours before being examined, possibly exposing many people to an infectious virus. If a patient appears

SOURCE: Katie Walter, "Diagnosing Flu Fast," *Science and Technology Review,* December 2006, pp. 5–9. Reprinted by permission of Lawrence Livermore National Laboratory.

to need more than the routine fluids-and-rest prescription, effective diagnosis requires tests that must be sent to a laboratory. Hours or days may pass before results are available to the doctor, who in the meantime must make an educated guess about the patient's illness. The lengthy diagnostic process places a heavy burden on medical laboratories and can result in improper use of antibiotics or a costly hospital stay.

A faster testing method may soon be available. An assay [analysis] developed by a team of Livermore scientists can diagnose influenza and other respiratory viruses in about two hours once a sample has been taken. Unlike other systems that operate this quickly, the new device, called $FluID_X$ (and pronounced "fluidics"), can differentiate five types of respiratory viruses, including influenza. $FluID_X$ can analyze samples at the point of patient care—in hospital emergency departments and clinics—allowing medical providers to quickly determine how best to treat a patient, saving time and potentially thousands of dollars per patient.

The $FluID_X$ project, which is led by Livermore chemist Mary McBride of the Physics and Advanced Technologies Directorate, received funding from the National Institute of Allergy and Infectious Diseases and the Laboratory Directed Research and Development (LDRD) Program. To test the system and make it as useful as possible, the team worked closely with the Emergency Department staff at the University of California (UC) at Davis Medical Center in Sacramento. Robert Derlet, M.D. and chief of the department, is enthusiastic about having $FluID_X$ available for testing.

"A dozen or more viruses cause symptoms in people that all look the same in the early stages," says Derlet. "With most viruses, people are sick for just a few days and then get better. But flu and other respiratory viruses can make some people really sick and even kill them. We need to be able to sort out the 'bad guys' so these viruses don't infect others."

Increase in Vaccination Rates 2008–2010

2008–09 Flu Season

33% — Adults vaccinated

34% — Children vaccinated

2009–10 Flu Season

40% — Adults vaccinated

40% — Children vaccinated

Taken from: Centers for Disease Control and Prevention, "More Americans Got Seasonal Flu Vaccination in 2009–2010 Than in Previous Years," April 29, 2010.

Rapid Virus Identification Is Needed

Flu kills more than 35,000 people every year in the U.S. The 2003 outbreak of severe acute respiratory syndrome and the ongoing concern about a possible bird flu pandemic illustrate the need for a fast, reliable test that can differentiate seasonal flu from a potentially pandemic influenza. Such a test should also discriminate influenza from pathogens that cause illnesses with flulike symptoms.

When a precise diagnosis is required to treat an adult patient with serious respiratory symptoms, sample cells are usually obtained with a nasal or throat swab and analyzed with one of several laboratory methods. The gold standard test is viral culturing, a highly sensitive method that can identify the specific strain of virus. However, viral culturing is a labor-intensive process and requires 3 to 10 days to produce results, far too long for early intervention. Enzyme and optical immunoassays offer results in 30 minutes, but these methods are less sensitive than viral culturing so they can produce false positives or negatives. They also cannot distinguish the type of virus found.

Direct immunofluorescence antibody (DFA) staining is as sensitive as viral culturing. It also can detect multiple respiratory pathogens simultaneously by a process known as multiplexing. However, DFA staining requires expensive equipment, a skilled microscopist, and samples with enough target cells for testing. In addition, the results are ultimately subjective. Another method, called reverse transcriptase-polymerase chain reaction assay, offers sensitivity and specificity comparable to viral culturing and DFA staining. It also produces results in two hours and can rapidly test a large number of samples. The drawback with these tests, however, is that they must be performed in a laboratory. None of them can be used where they are needed most: in the clinic or emergency department where patients are being treated.

Livermore's FluID$_X$ diagnostic system, with its instrumentation and multiplexed assays, is designed specifically for point-of-care diagnosis. The fast, easy-to-use system is based on the Autonomous Pathogen Detection System, a homeland security technology developed by Lawrence Livermore. This R&D 100 Award–winning technology constantly monitors the air to detect airborne bioterrorism agents, such as anthrax.

FluID$_X$ is an integrated system designed to perform highly multiplexed polymerase chain reaction (PCR) nucleic-acid-based assays in real time. The FluID$_X$ system processes a sample, analyzes the data, reports the results, and decontaminates itself before another sample is taken. The device currently uses 16 assays—12 for individual nucleic-acid targets and 4 for internal controls. The assays can simultaneously detect influenza A and B,

In 2009 the Analytik Jena AG company in Germany developed a new rapid test for the H1N1 virus that can detect an H1N1 virus infection in less than two hours. (**AP Images/ Jens Meyer**)

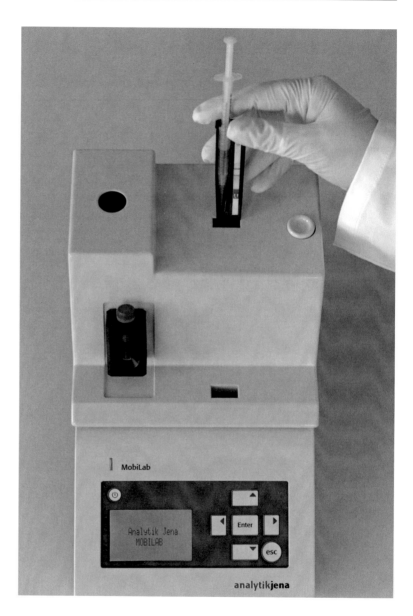

parainfluenza (Types 1 and 3), respiratory syncytial virus, and adenovirus (Groups B, C, and E). . . .

Validated by Tests

In tests of FluID$_X$, a technician at the UC Davis Medical Center collected more than 1,200 nasal swab samples from patients seeking treatment in the Emergency Department. As part of the federal requirements for research involving human subjects, study participants signed informed consent forms before samples were taken, and the testing protocol was approved by UC Davis physicians and the governing Institutional Review Board.

Nasal swabs were also collected from volunteers who showed no signs of illness. All samples were processed using viral culturing, DFA staining, and FluID$_X$. Sample comparisons revealed excellent results for FluID$_X$. In terms of sensitivity, the FluID$_X$ multiplexed assays were on par with the results from viral culturing. The system's specificity for identifying virus strains was significantly better than that obtained with DFA staining, which takes about the same time as FluID$_X$ . . . .

The team continues to improve the assays and is working to automate a stand-alone device. The LDRD Program is supporting assay development to expand the FluID$_X$ panel. Device testing will continue at the Emergency Department of the UC Davis Medical Center until June 2007. If additional funding is awarded, the team will build several next-generation systems with 10 separate (parallel) PCR reaction chambers to enable asynchronous sample processing. Asynchronous processing will, in turn, allow sample throughput that is better aligned with the requirements of busy hospitals, especially during the influenza season or in the event of a pandemic influenza.

The flu season arrives every year without fail, bringing fever, coughing, and runny noses. Soon perhaps, FluID$_X$ will be a workhorse application, helping doctors decide how best to care for their patients.

Next-Generation Flu Vaccines Are Emerging

Teddi Dineley Johnson

Flu vaccine has traditionally been produced in hen's eggs. This method works, but not efficiently. In the following selection science writer Teddi Dineley Johnson describes efforts to develop new flu vaccines by using new techniques. Mammalian cells are being coaxed into nurturing flu viruses that can be harvested for vaccines. Other researchers are experimenting with genetically modified viruses that contain flu genes but are infectious only to insects. The federal government is supporting such efforts, Johnson reports, because it sees an urgent need for the nation to be able to produce new vaccines quickly in case of a new epidemic. Johnson is a public affairs and advocacy reporter for the *Nation's Health*.

With the reliability of a finely tuned clock, seasonal influenza returns each year, causing about 36,000 U.S. deaths and incalculable misery. Not as reliable has been the availability of the most important tool for controlling flu: vaccines.

SOURCE: Teddi Dineley Johnson, "Next Generation of Flu Vaccines Coming of Age," *Nation's Health,* vol. 40, no. 1, February 2010. Reprinted by permission.

Delays, shortages and distribution problems that have stymied immunization efforts in recent years have raised questions about the nation's commitment to preparedness and sparked interest in the government's efforts to develop new and better flu vaccines. Without compromising efficacy and safety, greater innovation is needed in the area of vaccine development, said a December [2009] Institute of Medicine [IoM] report.

"Developing and manufacturing most vaccines involves using living organisms and presents unique technical and regulatory challenges," said the report, *Priorities for the National Vaccine Plan.*

Both industry and regulators are "risk averse," the report said, noting that progress in regulatory science in general has been slow and as a result, a "tried and true paradigm" characterizes some aspects of vaccine development and regulation.

One such paradigm, the half-century-old egg-based method of producing flu vaccine, has major limitations, experts say, including a lengthy six- to nine-month manufacturing process and the need to forecast and select the virus strains to be used in the vaccine at least six months ahead of the flu season, not to mention the annual demand for hundreds of millions of fertilized chicken eggs. Also, decisions about which viral strains to include in the vaccine may not always be correct, and midcourse corrective action is virtually impossible because of the long lead time required to acquire eggs. Also concerning is the fact that people who are allergic to eggs cannot receive the vaccine.

"We need a better technology for making flu vaccine," Arthur Reingold, MD, a member of the IoM report's authoring committee, told *The Nation's Health.* "People have recognized that, and there is good work going on."

> ## FAST FACT
>
> Wired.com reports that a new vaccine under development causes antibodies to go after a piece of protein that is stable across many different flu viruses. It It is hoped it will prove to be a universal flu vaccine.

New Methods Are Needed

The Institute of Medicine released its report on the same day that the National Institutes of Health hosted an educational seminar for the media on new flu vaccine technologies. In an event speech, Health and Human Services [HHS] Secretary Kathleen Sebelius told attendees that the process used to make the egg-based flu vaccine is "cumbersome and outdated."

"We couldn't have had a better indication of the need for new flu vaccine technology than our experience with the 2009 H1N1 virus this fall," Sebelius said. "It will be several more years before we are able to wean ourselves away from egg-based vaccine, but we are committed to move ahead with 21st century vaccine development."

Demonstrating her commitment to new flu vaccine technologies, Sebelius was present in late November [2009] when Novartis Vaccines and Diagnostics cut the ribbon on the nation's first large-scale U.S. facility to manufacture cell-based vaccine for seasonal and pandemic flu. In place of eggs, the nearly $1 billion Holly Springs, N.C., plant is using laboratory-grown mammalian cells that are capable of hosting a growing virus. Cell culture–based vaccines are already approved for use in some European countries.

Because cell-based influenza vaccine can be made faster and in greater quantities than traditional vaccine, the new facility is expected to increase the nation's capacity to make pandemic influenza vaccine by at least 25 percent, according to HHS, which awarded Novartis a $487 million multi-year contract to support the initiative's domestic manufacturing capacity.

The plant is expected to be running at full-scale commercial production in 2013 and will also be producing the company's proprietary adjuvant. When injected together with a vaccine, adjuvants expand and compound the strength of the response to allow for a lesser dose of the vaccine.

Marking another bold move into the future, HHS in June awarded Protein Sciences of Meriden, Conn., an initial $35 million contract to develop a so-called recombinant influenza vaccine. Under the technology, a gene is extracted from a flu virus and placed into an insect virus called baculovirus, which does not affect people but can multiply quickly to high levels in insect cells. The cells are purified to become a basic part of a human vaccine. Using this method, vaccine production may be available faster than by using traditional egg-based production methods, and because the basic cells can be frozen and stored indefinitely, manufacturing large quantities of a vaccine would also be faster, according to a statement released in June by HHS.

Health and Human Services secretary Kathleen Sebelius gives a thumbs up to a child who is about to get the new H1N1 vaccine. Sebelius is committed to developing non-egg-based vaccines. (**Roger L. Wollenberg/UPI/ Landov**)

Other new technologies for producing influenza vaccines include DNA-based approaches and the development of broadly protective "universal" vaccines based on influenza virus proteins that are shared by multiple strains.

One strategy to produce improved influenza vaccine is at the finish line and will likely be available for the 2010–2011 flu season. In December, the Food and Drug Administration approved Sanofi Pasteur's licensed application for a high-dose flu vaccine aimed at seniors. According to a company statement, the vaccine is specifically designed to generate a more robust immune response in people 65 and older, an age group that "typically does not respond as well to the standard dose of influenza virus vaccines as younger individuals because they have weakened immune systems."

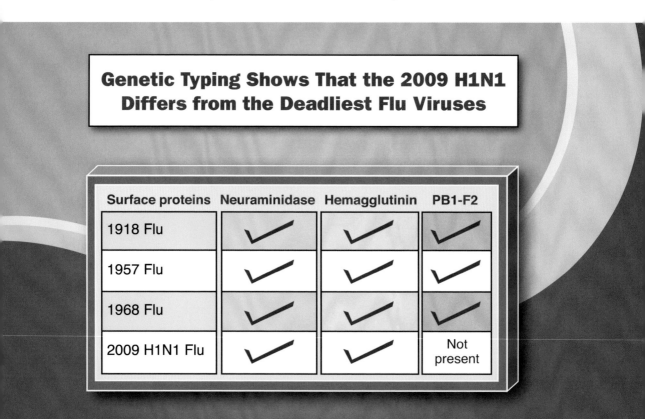

Genetic Typing Shows That the 2009 H1N1 Differs from the Deadliest Flu Viruses

Surface proteins	Neuraminidase	Hemagglutinin	PB1-F2
1918 Flu	✓	✓	✓
1957 Flu	✓	✓	✓
1968 Flu	✓	✓	✓
2009 H1N1 Flu	✓	✓	Not present

Taken from: Tina Hesman Saey, "Swine Flu Lacks Killer Molecule," *Wired Science*, June 15, 2010.

Transitioning to newer methods has been slow, partly because the development and production of vaccine is fundamentally a private-sector issue, said Anthony S. Fauci, MD, director of the National Institute of Allergy and Infectious Diseases. Incentives for private companies to invest in the transition from the established methodology of developing flu vaccines in eggs have been few, especially because vaccine—and flu vaccine in particular—is not a big profit maker for companies.

"There is a risk when you're dealing with needing to grow the virus in the medium of eggs that something could go wrong, namely the virus can grow slow, the situation can require a surge of many more doses than you thought you would need, and it is difficult to, on a dime, start surging with more doses because you have to preorder the chickens, preorder the eggs, preinoculate the eggs, etc.," Fauci told *The Nation's Health*. "So there was always the realization that this was a fragile system. It worked and it has worked for decades but the incentive to transition into a more modern, reliable and surgable technique was not there."

Teamwork Is Essential

Recent threats, such as H5N1 avian influenza—which continues to smolder—reinforced the need for the federal government to partner with private sector companies and help them shift development to new cell culture technologies, Fauci said.

"However, that process doesn't happen overnight," Fauci said, noting that it takes years to build factories and show that a virus can grow in cells and that a vaccine is safe and effective. "That process was already ongoing when we became aware that we needed to make a vaccine for H1N1. It was ongoing but not quite ready for prime time, so right now we are seeing that transition get closer and closer to reality."

The transition from eggs to cells speeds the vaccine manufacturing process by several weeks, Fauci said, and offers more flexibility in terms of being able to "surge up" with many more doses. But the new technology is not the final frontier by any means.

"I don't consider, nor do many of my colleagues consider, that that's the end game solution," Fauci said, pointing to what he calls the "ultimate holy grail"—a universal vaccine that would theoretically provide protection against any strain of influenza without needing to be updated or administered every year to protect against newly emerging annual or pandemic strains, but "that is years away," he said.

CHAPTER 2

Controversies About Influenza

Flu Outbreaks Are Caused by a Drop in Humidity

Public Library of Science

It has long been observed that the number of flu cases rises in the winter, but the reasons have been a matter of speculation. In the following selection the Public Library of Science offers a research-based view that the drop in humidity that accompanies cold weather accounts for the seasonal rise in influenza. Jeffrey Shaman, the lead author in the study, says that in reviewing more than thirty years of data, the research team found a correlation between the drop in humidity and the rise in the number of flu cases. Scientists involved in the study believe that lower humidity increases the survival rate of the flu virus outside the body, facilitating contagion. The Public Library of Science is a nonprofit organization of scientists and physicians that works to provide unlimited access to the latest scientific research, as well as to enable scientists, librarians, publishers, and entrepreneurs to develop innovative ways to explore and use the world's treasury of scientific ideas and discoveries.

Photo on previous page. In an effort to curb the spread of swine flu in China, police officers drive pigs infected with swine flu to a slaughterhouse. Farming practices have been widely blamed for several swine flu outbreaks. (**AP Images/ Peng Tong.**)

SOURCE: Public Library of Science, "Dry Winters Linked to Seasonal Outbreaks of Influenza," *ScienceDaily*, February 23, 2010. Reprinted by permission.

The seasonal increase of influenza has long baffled scientists, but a new study published in *PLoS Biology* has found that seasonal changes of absolute humidity are the apparent underlying cause of these wintertime peaks. The study also found that the onset of outbreaks might be encouraged by anomalously dry weather conditions, at least in temperate regions.

Scientists have long suspected a link between humidity and seasonal (epidemic) flu outbreaks, but most of the research has focused on relative humidity—the ratio of water vapor content in the air to the saturating level, which varies with temperature. Absolute humidity quantifies the actual amount of water in the air, irrespective of temperature. Though somewhat counter-intuitive, absolute humidity is much higher in the summer. "In some areas of the country, a typical summer day can have four times as much water vapor as a typical winter day—a difference that exists both indoors and outdoors," said Jeffrey Shaman, an Oregon State University atmospheric scientist and lead author.

Long-Term Observation Yields Findings

The researchers used 31 years of observed absolute humidity conditions to drive a mathematical model of influenza and found that the model simulations reproduced the observed seasonal cycle of influenza throughout the United States. They first examined influenza in New York, Washington, Illinois, Arizona and Florida, and found that the absolute humidity conditions in those states all produced model-simulated seasonal outbreaks of influenza that correlated well with the observed seasonal cycle of influenza within each state. Shaman and colleagues then extended their model to the rest of the continental U.S. and were able to reproduce the seasonal cycle of influenza elsewhere. They also discovered that the start of many influenza outbreaks during the winter was directly preceded by a period of weather that was drier than usual.

Scientists have long suspected the existence of a link between humidity and seasonal flu outbreaks. A recent study has found that it is not uncommon for flu outbreaks to be preceded by a period of drier weather than is typical. (© Chuck Pefley/Alamy)

"This dry period is not a requirement for triggering an influenza outbreak, but it was present in 55 to 60 percent of the outbreaks we analyzed so it appears to increase the likelihood of an outbreak," said Shaman. "The virus response is almost immediate; transmission and survival rates increase and about 10 days later, the observed influenza mortality rates follow."

Other Factors Cloud Forecasts

Though the findings by Shaman and his colleagues build a strong case for absolute humidity's role in influenza outbreaks, it does not mean you can predict where influenza will strike next. As Shaman emphasized, "Certainly absolute humidity may affect the survival of the influenza virus, but the severity of outbreaks is also dependent upon other variables, including the type of virus and its virulence, as well as host-mediated factors such as the susceptibility of a population and rates of population mixing and person-to-person interactions."

Marc Lipsitch, a professor of epidemiology at the Harvard School of Public Health and senior author on the new study, said the new analysis may have implications for other diseases. "Seasonality of infectious diseases is one of the oldest observations in human health, but the mechanisms—especially for respiratory diseases like flu—have been unclear," Lipsitch said. "This study, in combination with Shaman and (Melvin) Kohn's earlier analysis of laboratory experiments on flu transmission, points to variation in humidity as a major cause of seasonal cycles in flu."

> **FAST FACT**
>
> A 2007 study at Mount Sinai Medical School in New York City found that when guinea pigs were exposed to an airborne flu virus at different cage temperatures and humidity levels, the rates of infection varied significantly.

"Seasonal variation in flu, in turn, helps to explain variation in other infectious diseases—such as pneumococcal and meningococcal disease—as well as seasonal variation in heart attacks, strokes and other important health outcomes."

Findings May Help Limit Outbreaks

Lipsitch directs the Center for Communicable Disease Dynamics, of which Shaman is a member. This study and the center are supported by the Models of Infectious Disease Agent Study, or "MIDAS Program," of the U.S. National Institute of General Medical Sciences.

"The discovery of a link between influenza outbreaks and absolute humidity could have a major impact on the development of strategies for limiting the spread of infection," said Irene Eckstrand, who oversees the MIDAS program. "Understanding why outbreaks arise is an important first step toward containing or even preventing

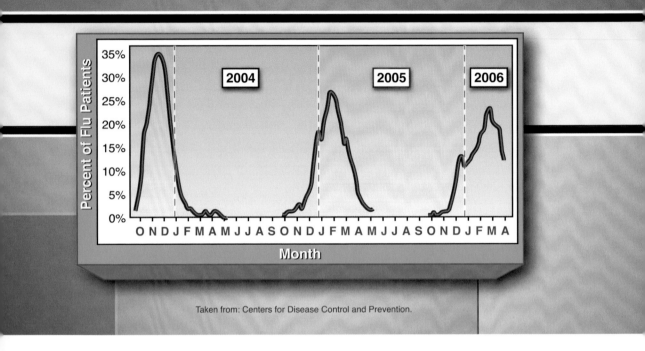

US Flu Season Peaks in Winter, When Humidity Is Low

2004   2005   2006

Taken from: Centers for Disease Control and Prevention.

them, so it is essential for scientists to follow up on this intriguing connection."

Additional collaborators on the study published in *PLoS Biology* were Virginia Pitzer and Bryan Grenfell, Princeton University; and Cecile Viboud, National Institutes of Health, Fogarty International Center. The study builds on previous laboratory research that found influenza virus survival rates increased greatly as absolute humidity decreased.

Avian Flu Threatens Human Life

Centers for Disease Control and Prevention

Avian flu is commonplace among birds. Occasionally, it jumps the species barrier to infect humans. In the following selection the Centers for Disease Control and Prevention (CDC) documents instances of avian flu attacking people. Many of the cases occur in Asia, where small poultry farms are commonplace. Although most people survive the avian flu, the CDC reports a number of fatalities. The selection concludes with a warning to people who work with poultry to take protective measures. The Atlanta-based CDC is a part of the US Department of Health and Human Services. The CDC is the primary federal agency responsible for monitoring the spread of communicable disease and coordinating prevention and response to outbreaks.

Although avian influenza A viruses usually do not infect humans, rare cases of human infection with avian influenza A viruses have been reported. Most human infections with avian influenza

SOURCE: Centers for Disease Control and Prevention, "Avian Flu: A Virus Infections of Humans," May 23, 2008. Reprinted by permission.

A viruses have occurred following direct contact with infected poultry. Human clinical illness from infection with avian influenza A viruses has ranged from eye infections (conjunctivitis) to severe respiratory disease (pneumonia) to death.

Since November 2003, nearly 400 cases of human infection with highly pathogenic avian influenza A (H5N1) viruses have been reported by more than a dozen countries in Asia, Africa, the Pacific, Europe and the Near East. Highly pathogenic avian influenza A (H5N1) viruses have never been detected among wild birds, domestic poultry, or people in the United States. The World Health Organization (WHO) maintains situation updates and cumulative reports of human cases of avian influenza A (H5N1). Most human cases of H5N1 virus infection are thought to have occurred as a result of direct contact with sick or dead infected poultry.

Other subtypes of avian influenza A viruses also have infected humans, including low pathogenic and highly pathogenic virus strains. Public health authorities closely monitor outbreaks of human illness associated with avian influenza because of concerns about the potential for more widespread infection in the human population. The spread of avian influenza A viruses from one ill person to another has been reported very rarely, and has been limited, inefficient and unsustained. However, because avian influenza A viruses have the potential to change and gain the ability to spread easily between people, monitoring for human infection and person-to-person transmission is important.

Poultry Outbreak

Avian influenza outbreaks among poultry occur worldwide from time to time. Since 1997, for example, and based on the World Organization for Animal Health (OIE) reporting criteria for Notifiable Avian Influenza in

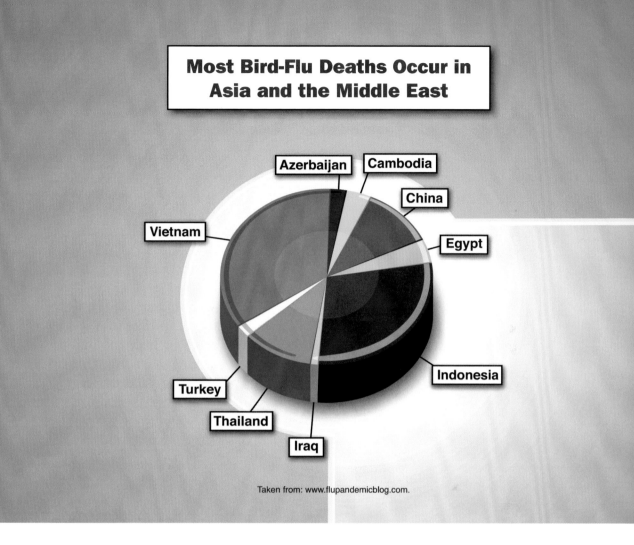

Most Bird-Flu Deaths Occur in Asia and the Middle East

Azerbaijan

Cambodia

China

Vietnam

Egypt

Turkey

Indonesia

Thailand

Iraq

Taken from: www.flupandemicblog.com.

commercial poultry, the United States has experienced 17 incidents of H5 and H7 low pathogenic avian influenza (LPAI), and one incident of highly pathogenic avian influenza (HPAI) that was restricted to one poultry farm. The U.S. Department of Agriculture monitored and responded to these incidents.

In 2004, the United States experienced the first highly pathogenic avian influenza outbreak among poultry in 20 years. This was an outbreak of avian influenza A (H5N2) which occurred in Texas. The outbreak was reported in a flock of 7,000 chickens in south-central Texas. There was no report of transmission to humans. . . .

Human Cases

Confirmed instances of avian influenza A virus infections of humans since 1996 include:

- H7N7, United Kingdom, 1996: One adult developed conjunctivitis after a piece of straw contacted her eye while cleaning a duck house. Low pathogenic avian influenza A (H7N7) virus was isolated from a conjunctiva specimen. The person was not hospitalized and recovered.
- H5N1, Hong Kong, Special Administrative Region, 1997: Highly pathogenic avian influenza A (H5N1) virus infections occurred in both poultry and humans. This was the first time an avian influenza A virus transmission directly from birds to humans had been found to cause respiratory illness. During this outbreak, 18 people were hospitalized and six of them died. To control the outbreak, authorities culled about 1.5 million chickens to remove the source of the virus. The most significant risk factor for human H5N1 illness was visiting a live poultry market in the week before illness onset.
- H9N2, China and Hong Kong, Special Administrative Region, 1999: Low pathogenic avian influenza A (H9N2) virus infection was confirmed in two hospitalized children and resulted in uncomplicated influenza-like illness. Both patients recovered, and no additional cases were confirmed. The source is unknown. Several additional human H9N2 virus infections were reported from China in 1998–99.
- H7N2, Virginia, 2002: Following an outbreak of low pathogenic avian influenza A (H7N2) among poultry in the Shenandoah Valley poultry production area, one person developed uncomplicated influenza-like illness and had serologic evidence of infection with H7N2 virus.
- H5N1, China and Hong Kong, Special Administrative Region, 2003: Two cases of highly pathogenic avian

influenza A (H5N1) virus infection occurred among members of a Hong Kong family that had traveled to China. One person recovered, the other died. How or where these two family members were infected was not determined. Another family member died of a respiratory illness in China, but no testing was done.

- H7N7, Netherlands, 2003: The Netherlands reported outbreaks of highly pathogenic avian influenza A (H7N7) virus among poultry on multiple farms. Overall, 89 people were confirmed to have H7N7 virus infections associated with poultry outbreaks. Most human cases occurred among poultry workers. H7N7-associated illness was generally mild and included 7 cases of conjunctivitis (eye infections); five cases of conjunctivitis and influenza-like illness with fever, cough, and muscle aches; two cases of influenza-like illness; and four cases that were classified as "other." One death occurred in a veterinarian who visited one of the affected farms and developed complications from H7N7 virus infection, including acute respiratory distress syndrome. The majority of H7N7 cases occurred through direct contact with infected poultry. However, Dutch authorities reported three possible instances of human-to-human H7N7 virus transmission from poultry workers to family members.

- H9N2, Hong Kong, Special Administrative Region, 2003: Low pathogenic avian influenza A (H9N2) virus infection was confirmed in a child in Hong Kong. The child was hospitalized with influenza-like illness and recovered.

- H7N2, New York, 2003: In November 2003, a patient with serious pre-existing medical conditions was admitted to a hospital in New York with respiratory symptoms. The patient recovered and went home after a few weeks. Testing revealed that the patient had been infected with a low pathogenic avian influenza A (H7N2) virus; the patient's underlying medical conditions likely contributed to the severity of the patient's illness.

- H7N3, Canada, 2004: In March 2004, two poultry workers who were assisting in culling operations during a large influenza (H7N3) poultry outbreak had culture-confirmed H7N3 conjunctivitis, one of whom also had coryza. Both poultry workers recovered. One worker was infected with low pathogenic H7N3 and the other with high pathogenic H7N3.

- H5N1, China, Thailand and Vietnam, 2003–2004: In late 2003 and early 2004, severe and fatal human infections with highly pathogenic avian influenza A (H5N1) viruses were associated with widespread poultry outbreaks. Most cases had pneumonia and many had respiratory failure. Additional human H5N1 cases were reported during mid-2004, and late 2004. Most cases appeared to be associated with direct contact with sick or dead poultry. One instance of possible, limited, human-to-human spread of H5N1 virus is believed to have occurred in Thailand. Overall, 50 human H5N1 cases with 36 deaths were reported from three countries.

- H5N1, Cambodia, China, Indonesia, Thailand, Vietnam, 2005: Severe and fatal human infections with highly pathogenic avian influenza A (H5N1) viruses were associated with the ongoing H5N1 epizootic among poultry in the region. Overall, 98 human H5N1 cases with 43 deaths were reported from five countries.

- H5N1, Azerbaijan, Cambodia, China, Djibouti, Egypt, Indonesia, Iraq, Thailand, Turkey, 2006: Severe and fatal human infections with highly pathogenic avian influenza A (H5N1) viruses occurred in association with the ongoing and expanding epizootic. While most of these cases occurred as a result of contact with infected poultry, in Azerbaijan, the most plausible cause of exposure to H5N1 in several instances of human infection is thought to be contact with infected dead wild birds (swans). The largest family cluster of H5N1 cases to date occurred in North Sumatra, Indonesia during May 2006, with seven confirmed H5N1 cases and one probable H5N1 case, including seven deaths. Overall, 115 human H5N1 cases with 79 deaths were reported in nine countries.

- H5N1, Cambodia, China, Egypt, Indonesia, Laos, Myanmar, Nigeria, Pakistan, Vietnam, 2007: Severe and fatal human infections with highly pathogenic avian influenza A (H5N1) viruses occurred in association with poultry outbreaks. In addition, during 2007, Nigeria (January), Laos (February), Myanmar (December), and Pakistan (2007) confirmed their first human infections with H5N1. Overall nine countries reported a total of 86 human cases with 59 deaths in 2007.

- H7N2, United Kingdom, 2007: Human infection with low pathogenic avian influenza A (H7N2) virus resulting in influenza-like illness and conjunctivitis were

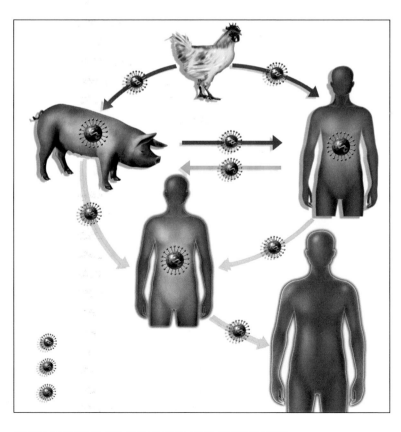

This illustration shows the recombination of the avian flu virus (red) with the human influenza virus (green) or swine influenza virus (green) that results in a new mutant virus that is very contagious and deadly to humans (blue). **(BSIP/Photo Researchers, Inc.)**

identified in four hospitalized cases. The cases were associated with an H7N2 poultry outbreak in Wales.

• H9N2, Hong Kong, Special Administrative Region, 2007: In March 2007, low pathogenic avian influenza A (H9N2) virus infection was confirmed in a 9-month-old Hong Kong girl with mild signs of disease. . . .

Symptoms and Treatment

The reported signs and symptoms of avian influenza in humans have ranged from eye infections (conjunctivitis) to influenza-like illness symptoms (e.g., fever, cough, sore throat, muscle aches) to severe respiratory illness (e.g. pneumonia, acute respiratory distress, viral pneumonia) sometimes accompanied by nausea, diarrhea, vomiting and neurologic changes.

CDC and WHO recommend oseltamivir, a prescription antiviral medication, for treatment and prevention of human infection with avian influenza A viruses. Analyses of available H5N1 viruses circulating worldwide suggest that most viruses are susceptible to oseltamivir. However, some evidence of resistance to oseltamivir has been reported in H5N1 viruses isolated from some human H5N1 cases. Monitoring for antiviral resistance among avian influenza A viruses is important and ongoing.

Persons who work with poultry or respond to avian influenza outbreaks among poultry and are therefore potentially exposed to infected or potentially infected poultry are advised to follow recommended biosecurity and infection control practices including careful attention to hand hygiene, and to use appropriate personal protective equipment. In addition, HPAI poultry outbreak responders should adhere to guidance from CDC and WHO and receive seasonal influenza vaccination and take prophylactic antiviral medication during an outbreak control response. Responders to LPAI outbreaks should consider this guidance as part

FAST FACT

In June 2010 a twenty-two-year-old pregnant Chinese woman died of the avian flu, becoming the first such fatality in more than a year.

of their response plan. Seasonal influenza vaccination will not prevent infection with avian influenza A viruses. Exposed persons should be carefully monitored for symptoms that develop during and in 7 days after their last exposure to infected poultry or to environments potentially contaminated with avian influenza A virus-excretions/secretions.

Swine Flu Is a Major Public Health Threat

President's Council of Advisors on Science and Technology

Addressing public health threats is an essential function of government. In 2009 the federal government identified H1N1 flu as a major threat. The following selection presents excerpts from a report to President Barack Obama prepared by the President's Council of Advisors on Science and Technology (PCAST). The report, issued in August 2009, terms H1N1 flu as "a serious health threat to the United States." It describes the so-called swine flu as falling midway between the catastrophic 1918 pandemic and the 1976 swine flu that failed to materialize. The council projects that up to ninety thousand Americans could die of H1N1 flu. It offers a number of recommendations to minimize the threat. PCAST is an advisory group of the nation's leading scientists and engineers, appointed by the president to augment the science and technology advice available to him from inside the White House and from cabinet departments and other federal agencies.

SOURCE: The President's Council of Advisors on Science and Technology, "Executive Report: US Preparations for 2009 H1N1 Influenza," August 7, 2009. Reprinted by permission.

In April 2009, a novel influenza A (H1N1) virus (2009-H1N1) appeared in Mexico, causing pneumonias and 59 deaths in Mexico City alone. The virus soon spread to the United States and to other continents. Within two months, the World Health organization (WHO) declared that the viral outbreak met the criteria of a level 6 pandemic. Although initial concerns of an extremely high fatality rate have receded, the expected resurgence of 2009-H1N1 in the fall poses a serious health threat to the United States.

Since the initial report of the outbreak, the Federal Government, through various departments, agencies, and offices, has been actively studying the course of events, responding to them, and planning for a resurgence of the pandemic this fall. In late June, President Obama requested that his Council of Advisors on Science and Technology (PCAST) undertake an evaluation of the 2009-H1N1 epidemic and the nation's response to a probable recurrence.

In this Executive Report, PCAST assesses the emerging Federal response to a second wave, identifies critical questions and gaps in this response, and suggests additional opportunities for mitigation. PCAST's observations, conclusions, and recommendations presented here are based on the analysis of its 2009-H1N1 Working Group, consisting of 3 PCAST members and a further 11 non-governmental experts in virology, public health, pediatrics, medicine, epidemiology, immunology, and other relevant scientific fields. The Working Group's deliberations were informed by discussions with government officials and others on various aspects of the 2009-H1N1 pandemic.

Historical Perspective

Based on the history of influenza pandemics over the past hundred years, PCAST places the current outbreak somewhere between the two extremes that have informed public opinion about influenza. On the one

In response to recommendations from his Council of Advisors on Science and Technology, President Barack Obama, right, outlines his administration's plans to combat H1N1 (swine) flu at a press conference in September 2009. At his side are Health and Human Services secretary Kathleen Sebelius and Education secretary Arne Duncan. (**AP Images/Charles Dharpak**)

hand, the 2009-H1N1 virus does not thus far seem to show the virulence associated with the devastating pandemic of 1918–19; moreover, medical science now has many potent tools at our disposal to mitigate an influenza pandemic in ways that were not possible ninety years ago. On the other hand, the 2009-H1N1 virus is a serious threat to our nation and the world, unlike the "swine flu" episode in 1976 that led to the vaccination of over 40 million Americans in the absence of any spread of the virus beyond an initial four cases at a single Army base.

Indeed, the 2009-H1N1 influenza is already responsible for significant morbidity and mortality world-wide—from its appearance in the spring, its continued circulation in the U.S. this summer [2009], and its spread through many countries in the Southern Hemisphere during their winter season. While the precise impact of the fall resurgence of 2009-H1N1 influenza is impossible to predict, a plausible scenario is that the epidemic could:

- produce infection of 30–50% of the U.S. population this fall and winter, with symptoms in approximately 20–40% of the population (60–120 million people), more than half of whom would seek medical attention.
- lead to as many as 1.8 million U.S. hospital admissions during the epidemic, with up to 300,000 patients requiring care in intensive care units (ICUs). Importantly, these very ill patients could occupy 50–100 percent of all ICU beds in affected regions of the country at the peak of the epidemic and could place enormous stress on ICU units, which normally operate close to capacity.
- cause between 30,000 and 90,000 deaths in the United States, concentrated among children and young adults. In contrast, the 30,000–40,000 annual deaths typically associated with seasonal flu in the United States occur mainly among people over 65. As a result, 2009-H1N1 would lead to many more years of life lost.
- pose especially high risks for individuals with certain pre-existing conditions, including pregnant women and patients with neurological disorders or respiratory impairment, diabetes, or severe obesity and possibly for certain populations, such as Native Americans. . . .

Risks and Recommendations

PCAST emphasizes that this is a planning scenario, not a prediction. But the scenario illustrates that an H1N1 resurgence could cause serious disruption of social and medical capacities in our country in the coming months. The circumstances underscore the importance of:

- ensuring that the nation's complex and distributed healthcare systems are prepared to deal with the potential surge in demand, especially with respect to critical care.
- ensuring that all feasible steps are taking to protect the most vulnerable populations.

Preparation for the predicted fall resurgence has been constrained by time and materials: the virus appeared in late spring and its resurgence is anticipated in early fall, while vaccine production currently requires at least 6 months. On the other hand, the development of preparedness plans was greatly stimulated by the recogni-

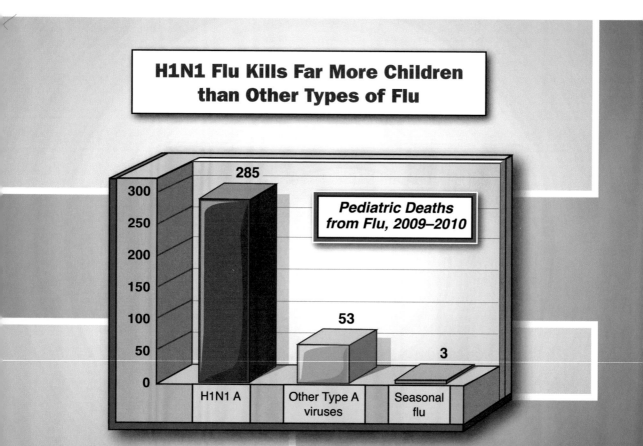

Taken from: Centers for Disease Control and Prevention 2009 H1N1 Flu Situation Update, "US Influenza-Associated Pediatric Mortality," May 28,2010./Influenza-Associated Pediatric Mortality Surveillance System.

tion a few years ago of the threat posed by a highly lethal avian influenza; preparations developed for this potential threat facilitated the response to the current, quite different strain of influenza virus.

PCAST is impressed by the efforts underway across our government—including the breadth and depth of thinking, energy being devoted, and awareness of potential pitfalls. The response is probably the best effort ever mounted against a pandemic, reflecting past preparedness efforts and the quality and commitment of the people involved.

Still, PCAST found some aspects of the decision-making and preparation processes that we believe could be improved, even in the short time remaining before the fall. These findings and recommendations are discussed at considerable length in its Working Group report.

Reflecting the rapid pace of response in the Federal Government, some of the suggested actions are already being considered, planned, or initiated by relevant agencies. In these cases, our recommendations are intended to provide support and additional focus to such efforts. Our recommendations fall into seven major categories:

1. Coordination. We suggest that coordination of the decision-makers could be more effectively orchestrated if a single person in the White House were assigned the responsibilities of clarifying decision-making authorities and processes, ascertaining that all important issues are resolved in a timely fashion, and reporting to you about actions to be taken.
2. Scenarios. We believe that preparations could be strengthened if the Federal Government developed and disseminated a few specific planning scenarios that Federal, state, local, and private entities could use to assess their capacities and plans for medical and non-medical interventions.

3. Surveillance. The ability to respond to the epidemic will depend on reliable and timely information about its course at the national, regional, and local level. We believe there are opportunities to make important upgrades to existing national surveillance systems in time for the expected fall resurgence.

4. Response. There are four critical pillars of a mitigation effort: vaccines, anti-viral drugs, medical care, and non-medical interventions that diminish virus spread. In particular, we focus on decisions that could reduce instances of severe disease and death by accelerating the delivery and use of vaccines; developing integrated plans to protect especially vulnerable populations; and ensuring access to intensive care facilities.

5. Barriers. Some legal, social, and financial barriers exist that may reduce compliance with some recommended measures for mitigation and we propose ways that the Federal Government and others could work to overcome such barriers.

6. Communication. Communication plans for relaying to the states, health workers, and the general public the government's recommended actions for mitigation are in some cases inadequate and should be strengthened.

7. Future Preparedness. The current outbreak highlights gaps in our capacity to combat epidemics caused by influenza and other agents. We outline steps that can be taken in the next few years, including improving vaccine production and design, anti-viral drug development, and health surveillance systems. . . .

Uncertainties and Concerns

The urgency of an ongoing pandemic, one that is likely to worsen in the next month or two, has compelled PCAST and its Working Group to perform its tasks rapidly. Under these circumstances, some of the information gathered by the Working Group for this report (such as the schedule for availability of vaccines and clinical data on infected individuals) must be viewed as provisional and subject to change.

Given the complexity of the situation and the many activities underway to deal with it, PCAST recognizes that the Working Group could not analyze the problem from every perspective and has doubtless failed to acknowledge all of the useful work that is already being done by members of the Obama Administration. In particular, the report does not rigorously address the measures that might need to be taken in the unlikely event that the pandemic proves to be much more severe than we currently envision.

PCAST hopes that its report and that of its Working Group help guide the urgent work that the Administration has undertaken to mitigate the effects of the 2009-H1N1 pandemic.

FAST FACT

Clinical Infectious Diseases reported in 2006 on a study finding that workers who are in frequent contact with pigs face greatly increased risk of swine influenza virus infection.

Swine Flu Is Not Likely to Be a Major Public Health Threat

Katharine Herrup

In 2009 the H1N1 flu, also known as swine flu, stirred panicky feelings after hundreds of people died of the disease in Asia and Mexico. However, in the following selection journalist Katharine Herrup says that when viewed in its proper perspective, the disease is not as fearsome as it might seem. Far more Americans die of heart disease and cancer, she points out, and the H1N1 pandemic is nowhere near as deadly as the 1918 Spanish flu pandemic. Moreover, she contends, only a tiny fraction of the flu deaths result from the disease alone. Most of its victims have preexisting conditions that render them vulnerable. So, while the H1N1 flu might become widespread, she writes, its fatality rate for healthy victims is unlikely to be significant. Herrup is a commentary editor for Reuters.com. She previously wrote an opinion column for the *New York Sun*.

SOURCE: Katharine Herrup, "You (Probably) Won't Die from Swine Flu: Putting H1N1 in Perspective," *Newsweek*, August 19, 2009. Reprinted by permission.

It seems like everyone is freaking out about the upcoming flu season [2009–2010] and the havoc H1N1 might wreak in America. Secretary of Health and Human Services Kathleen Sebelius says she's "preparing for the worst." Experts are worried vaccines won't be ready in time. Schools are contemplating quarantine situations. And the media is very concerned, judging by all the "Swine Flu—How Will It Affect Your Weekend?" stories each week.

But how worried should we really be? The facts *can* sound a little staggering: swine flu first hit the scene in late April, and by June 11, the World Health Organization declared swine flu a pandemic. The last flu pandemic declared was in 1967, 42 years ago—the Hong Kong flu, which killed about 700,000 people worldwide. So far, this swine flu is responsible for 1,462 deaths globally. Already, hundreds of thousands of people have contracted swine flu—so many that the WHO has stopped counting. In America, 447 people have died.

A little perspective shows that H1N1 isn't as scary as it sounds. Pandemic, with all its seemingly lethal connotations, simply means geographically widespread. The common cold, for instance, can always be classified as a pandemic.

Not as Bad as Feared

So far, the deadliness of swine flu pales in comparison to heart disease, cancer, and other flu pandemics like the Spanish flu of 1918, which wiped out 50 million people worldwide and the Asian flu of 1957–58, which killed about 2 million people. Furthermore, the swine flu appears to be behaving like a regular seasonal flu, with mild symptoms and many full recoveries.

That's not to say that the seasonal flu is harmless. It's the eighth-leading killer in America, with approximately 1 out of 5,000 dying from it. But deaths from the flu mostly occur because of complications like pneumonia or underlying chronic diseases like diabetes. Of the 56,326 people that died from the flu in America in 2006, only 849 of those deaths were caused directly by the flu, according to the Centers for Disease Control and Prevention, so if you're young and healthy—or even older and healthy—you're in good shape.

Heart disease, on the other hand, kills about 1 out of 50 people per year in America, which accounts for 26 percent of deaths in America annually. Cancer constitutes about 23 percent of America's yearly death toll, killing 559,888 people in 2006. The flu accounts for a measly 2.3 percent of deaths. Its death toll is just slightly higher than the number of people killed in auto accidents per year (43,664). Diabetes, stroke, Alzheimer's, accidents, emphysema and chronic bronchitis, hospital infections, even lung cancer are all more deadly than the swine flu (so far) and the seasonal flu. (Of course, you are more likely to die of H1N1 than being one of the roughly 37,286 per year that die of poisoning and other noxious substances or being one of the 38 randomly hit by lightning.) With what little data we have—remember, swine flu only hit the U.S. about five months ago—it's a safe bet that you probably won't die from swine flu.

Widespread Illness

But the odds are much better that you'll be sick with it: if 40 percent of the population does become infected with H1N1, more than 122 million people might contract swine flu. "What makes flu so bad is that it infects so many people," says Dr. Martin Blaser, chairman of the Department of Medicine at NYU Langone Medical Center, be it swine, bird, or regular sick-kid-on-the-schoolbus flu.

H1N1 is spreading more quickly than the seasonal flu, in part because most people haven't built up an immunity to this new strain of virus. The [flu is] also targeting

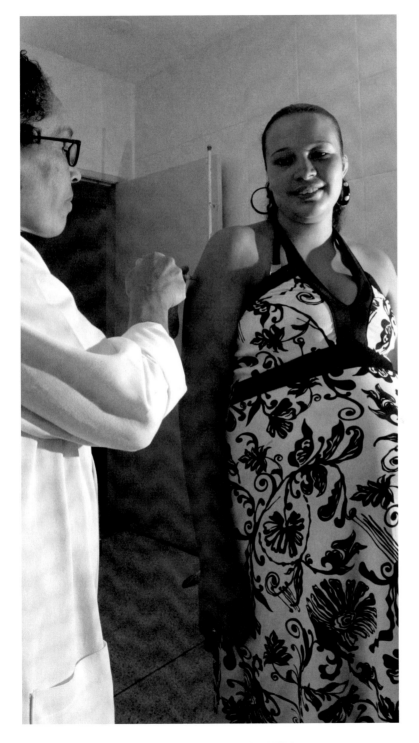

A pregnant woman receives an H1N1 vaccination as part of a Brazilian program to vaccinate all pregnant women in the country. Pregnant women and children are the most susceptible to contracting swine flu. (AP Images/Renato Conde)

a much younger, healthier age group. Typically, the large majority of people killed by the flu are those 65 years and older. However, the swine flu has been more prevalent among pregnant women and young adults. Currently, 6 percent of swine-flu deaths worldwide have occurred in healthy, pregnant women, compared with very rare occurrences with regular flu deaths. Even though mortality will stay low, "the social impacts of the deaths will be greater because it produces death among younger people," says Dr. Jarbas Barbosa, the Pan American Health Organization's regional adviser in immunization and vaccines.

> **FAST FACT**
>
> In mid-2009 the global fatality rate for H1N1 flu was estimated at under 0.5 percent, or fewer than one in two hundred cases.

In Argentina, 20 to 25 percent of the population has been attacked by the flu over a three-week period. That could easily occur in the United States, where pandemics typically attack between 25 percent and 40 percent of the population. "If we get slammed with this massive burden of flu in a short period of time, even if the mortality rate is .01 percent, you'll feel more mortality," says Laurie Garrett, senior fellow for global health at the Council on Foreign Relations. "You'll have such overwhelmed medical systems that you will have people who will die because the systems are overwhelmed." (Luckily, the fact that swine flu hit in the off-season gave America time to prepare.)

Guarding Against Future Virulence

We can't know, with 100 percent certainty, how the flu will act once flu season kicks off this fall. "Swine flu is not deadly right now, but we don't know what it will become," says Stephen Morse, epidemiology professor at Columbia University's School of Public Health. "Most believe that this is likely to come back during flu season and be more severe." But for now, the statistics offer some safety.

And while it's always good sense to wash your hands and not cough on strangers, there's no need to break out the protective masks and quarantine kit quite yet. Instead, hit the gym, eat some fiber, and wear your seat belt.

Benefits of the Flu Vaccine Outweigh the Risks

Debora MacKenzie

The flu is a serious, sometimes deadly, viral disease. In the following selection science writer Debora MacKenzie presents evidence that the dangers of flu exceed the hazards of the flu vaccine. Much of the fear of the flu vaccine stems from an outbreak of the paralyzing Guillain-Barré syndrome that followed mass flu vaccinations in 1976. While acknowledging that twenty-five people succumbed to vaccine-related complications, MacKenzie points out that in relation to the numbers vaccinated, very few died or were injured. Furthermore, she says, the flu itself causes a greater incidence of the same syndrome than the vaccine. There are some legitimate reasons to worry about vaccines, but on the whole, she argues, people are safer with them. MacKenzie is a science journalist who writes regularly for *New Scientist* and other publications.

SOURCE: Debora MacKenzie, "Swine Flu Myth: The Vaccine Isn't Safe—It Has Been Rushed Through Tests and the Last Time There Was a Swine Flu Scare the Vaccine Hurt People. Why Take the Risk to Prevent Mild Flu?," *New Scientist,* no. 2732, October 21, 2009. Reprinted by permission.

This flu isn't always mild and unlike ordinary flu it mostly kills young people, including the healthy. You might be one of the unlucky few. And even if you only get the mild version yourself, you might infect a family member or friend who then becomes severely ill. So doing nothing is risky, even if the odds are low.

What about the vaccines? People's nervousness about swine [H1N1] flu vaccines is understandable. In 1976, after the death of a US army recruit triggered fears of a repeat of the deadly 1918 pandemic, around 48 million Americans were given a swine flu vaccine. Of these, 532 developed Guillain-Barré syndrome, a paralytic condition caused by rogue antibodies attacking nerve cells. Most people recover from Guillain-Barré, but not all; 25 died after 1976 and others suffered lasting damage.

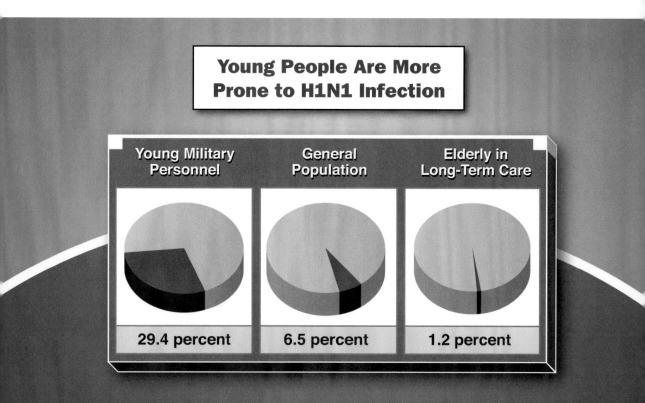

Young People Are More Prone to H1N1 Infection

Young Military Personnel	General Population	Elderly in Long-Term Care
29.4 percent	6.5 percent	1.2 percent

Taken from: *Journal of the American Medical Association,* April 13, 2010. http://jama.ama-assn.org.

Legacy of a Deadly Vaccine

The 1976 vaccine caused around 10 cases per million vaccinated. Even ordinary flu vaccines, however, are thought to cause one extra case of Guillain-Barré per million, in addition to the 10 to 20 per million who get Guillain-Barré some other way every year.

Does this mean it is safer not getting vaccinated? Absolutely not. First, there is the risk of swine flu killing you. Second, what few people know is that flu itself is far more likely to cause Guillain-Barré than any flu vaccine.

A 2009 study found that out of every million people who get flu, between 40 and 70 develop Guillain-Barré. So your best chance of avoiding Guillain-Barré is to get vaccinated, a conclusion backed by a 2007 study.

The vaccine risk is also diminishing. Cases of Guillain-Barré in the US have fallen 20 per cent since 1996, and cases reported after flu vaccination have fallen by 60 per cent. Intriguingly, this coincides with a fall in infections by the food poisoning bacterium *Campylobacter*, thanks to improved meat hygiene. Guillain-Barré usually follows infections, and *Campylobacter* is the main cause. It is also endemic among chickens, and flu vaccines are grown in chicken eggs. So the occasional contamination of flu vaccines with *Campylobacter* proteins might explain the link with Guillain-Barré, according to a 2004 study.

FAST FACT

The Centers for Disease Control and Prevention reports that life-threatening side effects of the flu vaccine are extremely rare.

Improvements in Vaccines

That is reassuring, if true. If the problem in 1976 was contamination rather than some property of the virus, there is no reason to expect a repeat. There has never been a similar problem with any other vaccine. And almost all the pandemic vaccines now being given in the US, the UK and Australia are being made in the same plants and in the same way as ordinary flu vaccines. Only two proteins on the vaccine virus have been changed, to match the 2009

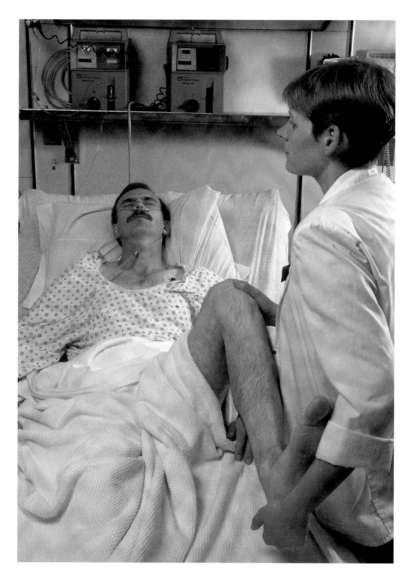

The 1976 swine flu vaccine was given to 48 million Americans. Of those, 532 people developed Guillain-Barré syndrome, a paralytic condition from which most people recovered. Many more people get the syndrome from the flu than from the vaccine. (**Will & Deni McIntyre/Photo Researchers, Inc.**)

H1N1 virus, and these proteins are similar to those of seasonal H1N1 flu, which have been in vaccines since 1977.

New Concerns

The exception is Celvapan. It contains the whole, killed pandemic virus, not a vaccine virus with pandemic proteins, and the virus is grown in cells rather than eggs—making it safe for people with egg allergy. While it and a similar bird flu vaccine have undergone safety testing, no seasonal flu vaccine has yet been made this way.

Another potential worry are the immune-stimulating chemicals called adjuvants that are added to some vaccines. The World Health Organization asked countries to make pandemic vaccines with adjuvants because much less of the key ingredient, dead flu virus, is needed per dose—meaning far more doses can be produced. The US could not do this because no seasonal flu vaccines with adjuvants had already been tested and approved there. In Europe they have been, so the main pandemic vaccines being given in Europe—Pandemrix (PDF) and Focetria—do contain adjuvants.

All the pandemic vaccines have had their own safety tests, and almost all are based on seasonal flu vaccines used for years. But very rare side effects can only be detected when millions take them. The seasonal flu vaccines with adjuvants have mostly been given to older people, so we cannot yet be sure that these vaccines do not have very rare side effects in younger people. Celvapan has had no large-scale monitoring. But here are some odds we do know about to consider.

The risk of getting Guillain-Barré from a flu vaccine is almost certainly less than 1 in a million; the risk of getting it from flu itself is more than 40 in a million. Swine flu is estimated to have killed 800 people in the US already, or more than 2 in every million so far. And during the first wave of swine flu this summer, 1 out of every 20,000 children aged 4 or under in the US ended up in hospital.

Still think it's safer not to get vaccinated?

Benefits of the Flu Vaccine Do Not Outweigh the Risks

Donald W. Miller Jr.

Vaccines are routine for most people. They begin in childhood and continue periodically. However, some people think that vaccines benefit their makers more than the people who receive them. In the following selection physician Donald W. Miller Jr. argues against the wisdom of getting a flu vaccination. Miller says the benefits of vaccination, while relatively greater than nonvaccination, are so small in absolute terms that they are not worth it. When the possible harms of vaccines are taken into consideration, he argues, the case against vaccination is solid. Miller is a cardiac surgeon and professor of surgery at the University of Washington in Seattle.

Another influenza season is beginning in the northern temperate zone, and our government's Centers for Disease Control and Prevention (CDC) will strongly urge Americans to get a flu shot. Health officials will say that every winter 5–20 percent of the population catches the flu, 200,000 people are hospitalized, and 36,000 people will die from it.

SOURCE: Donald W. Miller Jr., "Avoid Flu Shots, Take Vitamin D Instead," www.LewRockwell.com, October 3, 2008. Reprinted by permission.

The CDC's 15-member Advisory Committee on Immunization Practices (ACIP) makes recommendations each year on who should be vaccinated. Ten years ago, for the 1999–2000 season, the committee recommended that people over age 65 and children with medical conditions have a flu shot. Seventy-four million people were vaccinated. Next season (2000–01) the committee lowered the age for universal vaccination from 65 to 50 years old, adding 41 million people to the list. For the 2002–03 season, the ACIP added healthy children 6 months to 23 months old, and for 2004–05, children up to 5 years old. For the 2008–09 season the committee has advised that healthy children 6 months to 18 years old have a flu shot each year. Its recommendations for influenza vaccination now covers 256 million Americans—84 percent of the U.S. population. Only healthy people ages 19–49 not involved in some aspect of health care remain exempt. Pharmaceutical companies have made 146 million influenza vaccines for the U.S. market this flu season.

Conflicts of Interest

Almost all the ACIP members who make these recommendations have financial ties to the vaccine industry. The CDC therefore must grant each member a conflict-of-interest waiver.

The CDC mounts a well-orchestrated campaign each season to generate interest and demand for flu shots. Along with posters for the public, flyers, and health care provider materials, it encourages doctors to "recommend/urge flu shots." Medical groups, nonmedical organizations (like the YMCA), and the media trumpet CDC-released messages on influenza, notably: "Flu kills 36,000 per year," "This could be a bad/serious flu year," and "Flu vaccine is the best defense against flu." The government promotes National Vaccination Week, which this year [2008] is December 8–14. This year, however, rather

Vaccinated Physicians Tend to Vaccinate More of Their Patients

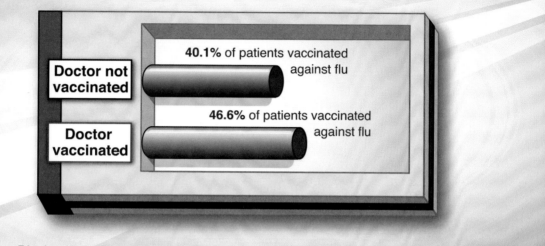

Doctor not vaccinated

40.1% of patients vaccinated against flu

Doctor vaccinated

46.6% of patients vaccinated against flu

Taken from: Yonatan Shapiro et al. "Higher Rates of Influenza Vaccination Among Patients of Vaccinated Physicians," Family Medical Practice Online. www.priory.com/fam.htm.

than uniformly following the government's "Seven-Step Recipe" for generating demand for flu shots, the mainstream media has questioned their benefits.

The *New York Times* had an article in the September 2, 2008 issue titled "Doubts Grow Over Flu Vaccine in Elderly," which says, "The influenza vaccine, which has been strongly recommended for people over 65 for more than four decades, is losing its reputation as an effective way to ward off the virus in the elderly. A growing number of immunologists and epidemiologists say the vaccine probably does not work very well for people over 70, the group that accounts for three-fourths of all flu deaths." The article refers to a study done by the Group Health Center for Health Studies in Seattle on 3,500 people, age 65–94, to determine if flu vaccines are effective in protecting older people against developing pneumonia.

Questionable Statistics

The *National Vital Statistics Reports* compiled by the CDC show that only 1,138 deaths a year occur due to influenza alone (257 in 2001, 727 in 2002, 1,792 in 2003, 1,100 in 2004, and 1,812 in 2005). Bacterial pneumonia causes some 60,000 deaths each year, mainly in the winter, when surveillance data show increased prevalence of the flu virus. Using a mathematical regression model, officials estimate that the flu virus triggers some of the winter-time deaths from pneumonia, along with deaths in people with cardiovascular disease and other chronic illnesses. More than 34,000 of those "36,000" flu deaths are what officials estimate are "influenza-associated" pneumonic and cardiovascular deaths.

The Group Health study reported in the *New York Times* and other newspapers around the country found that flu shots do *not* protect elderly people against developing pneumonia. Pneumonia occurs with equal frequency in people over age 65 with or without a flu shot. Earlier studies, biased by the "healthy user effect," overestimated the vaccine's effect on pneumonia because they did not adjust for the presence and severity of other diseases in unvaccinated people. As the Group Health authors point out, "The study found that people who were healthy and conscientious about staying well were the most likely to get an annual flu shot. Those who are frail may have trouble bathing or dressing on their own and are less likely to get to their doctor's office or a clinic to receive the vaccine. They are also more likely to be closer to death." Other investigators question that there is a mortality benefit with influenza vaccination. Vaccination coverage among the elderly increased from 15% in 1980 to 65% now, but there has been no decrease in deaths from influenza and pneumonia. As one vaccine researcher

> **FAST FACT**
>
> In November 2009 drug manufacturer GlaxoSmithKline recalled 170,000 doses of swine flu vaccines in Canada after adverse effects turned up at five times the predicted rate.

puts it, "I think the evidence base [for mortality benefits from flu shot] we have leaned on is not valid."

No Help to Children

There is also a lack of evidence that young children benefit from flu shots. A systematic review of 51 studies involving 260,000 children age 6 to 23 months found no evidence that the flu vaccine is any more effective than a placebo.

Randomized controlled trials are the most reliable way to determine the efficacy—and safety—of a given treatment. No randomized trials show that flu shots reduce mortality from influenza or flu-related pneumonia. Some do show that the flu vaccine is somewhat effective in preventing influenza. In one widely quoted study, 1,838 volunteers age 60 and over were randomized to receive a flu shot or placebo (a shot of saline). The flu shot reduced the *relative* risk of contracting (serologically confirmed, clinical) influenza by a seemingly impressive 50%. The incidence of influenza in the unvaccinated people in this study was 3%. In the vaccinated group it was 2%. Flu shots reduced the *absolute* risk of contracting influenza by a meager 1% (not 50%, as the "relative risk" portrays it). In actuality, for every 100 people that have a flu shot only one will benefit from it—this, in medical parlance, is the "number needed to treat" (NNT) in order to achieve any benefit from the treatment. A flu shot provides no benefit for the other 99 people—2 of them will get influenza anyway—and all 100 risk being harmed by the vaccine.

Another randomized trial . . . published recently found that the incidence of influenza in infants whose mothers had a flu shot during their pregnancy was 4% (6/159). The incidence of flu in infants whose mothers did not have a flu shot was 10% (16/157). In this study (done in Bangladesh and funded by the Bill and Melinda Gates Foundation, Wyeth Pharmaceuticals,

Some studies indicate that both in older adults and in babies whose pregnant mothers had been vaccinated, the flu vaccine is only minimally more effective than a placebo. (© **Bubbles Photolibrary/Alamy**)

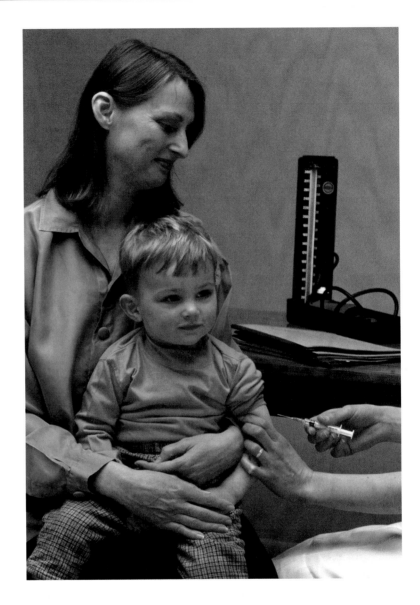

and others) flu shots reduced the relative risk of influenza illness in infants by a seemingly impressive 63%. But only 6 out of 100 infants benefited from the shot. The other 94 received no benefit—4 got influenza anyway—and all are at risk from being harmed by the vaccine, particularly from the mercury, aluminum, and formaldehyde in it.

Hazards in Vaccines

After officials select the three strains of flu virus that they think are most likely to be circulating during the next winter season (they picked the wrong ones last year), vaccine makers grow the viruses in fertilized chicken eggs, with 500,000 eggs per day (each examined by hand) for up to eight months. Formaldehyde is used to inactivate the virus. It is a known cancer-causing agent. Aluminum is added to promote an antibody response. It is a neurotoxin that may play a role in Alzheimer's disease. Other additives and adjuvants in the flu vaccine include Triton X-100 (a detergent), Polysorbate 80, carbolic acid, ethylene glycol (antifreeze), gelatin, and various antibiotics—neomycin, streptomycin, and gentamicin—that can cause allergic reactions in some people.

Two-thirds of the vaccines made for the 2008–09 flu season, 100 million of them, contain full-dose thimerosal, an organomercury compound, which is 49% mercury by weight. (An unidentified number of the other 50 million vaccines contain either "no" or "trace" amounts of thimerosal.) It is used to disinfect the vaccine. Each one of these 100 million flu shots contain 25 micrograms of mercury, a mercury content that is 50,000 parts per billion, 250 times more than the Environmental Protection Agency's safety limit. Mercury is a neurotoxin, which has a toxicity level 1,000 times that of lead.

There is some evidence that flu shots cause Alzheimer's disease. This most likely is a result of combining mercury with aluminum and formaldehyde, which renders them much more toxic together through a synergistic effect than each would be alone. One investigator has reported that people who received the flu vaccine each year for 3 to 5 years had a *ten-fold* greater chance of developing Alzheimer's disease than people who did not have any flu shots.

CHAPTER 3

Personal Experiences with Influenza

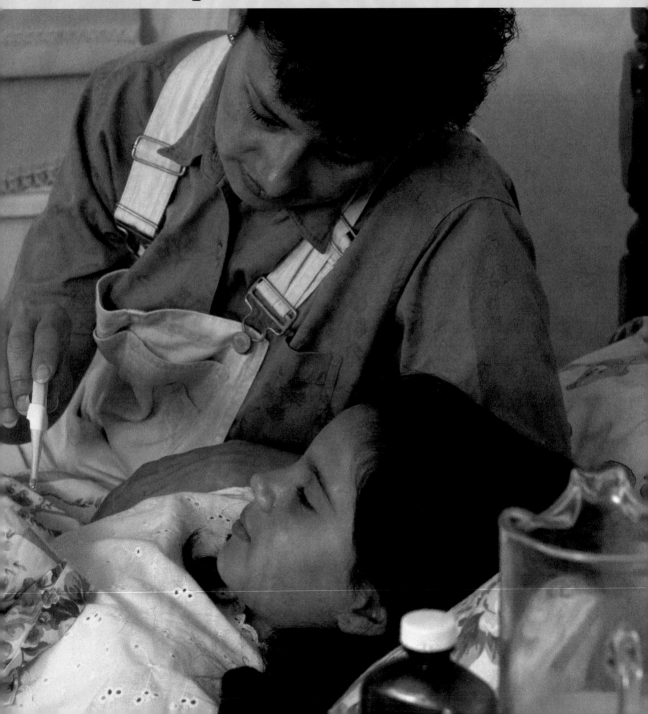

The Misery of Suffering Through Flu

Sarah Vine

When the flu hits, its effects can be devastating to the mind as well as the body. In the following selection journalist Sarah Vine gives a vivid account of her bout with swine flu. Before it struck, Vine had figured that if she got infected it would be nothing more than a mild illness. When it hit, however, the effect was overwhelming. She felt hot and cold at the same time and soon realized that she was hallucinating. Tamiflu, an antiviral medicine, made matters worse, and it was days before she recovered. Vine is a writer and editor at the *Times* of London.

A s I write, my brain feels as if it's rotating very gently, floating uncertainly inside the cavity of my skull. In my left ear, I can hear the faint, rhythmic rush of my pulse. My right ear is a blur of inflammation, the remnants of tonsillitis only just under control. When I swallow, pain catches in my throat, and I am still grinding my penicillin to stop the bitter pills from getting trapped

Photo on facing page. People who suffer from influenza feel miserable for about a week. **(Carolyn A. McKeone/Photo Researchers, Inc.)**

SOURCE: Sarah Vine, "My Swine Flu Misery," *Times Online* (London), July 22, 2009. Reprinted by permission.

in the doughy mass of inflamed tissue at the back of my mouth. Every now and again my heart does a little, inexplicable, flip in my chest, and if I walk upstairs I become unpleasantly warm and clammy.

And yet, compared with how I felt this time last week, I am in rude health. What's a little dizziness compared with the thumping pain of a headache that made even the softest pillow feel like a rough stone; or a bit of ear-fuzz after a throat so inflamed that swallowing water felt like imbibing shards of glass? No, I feel positively perky, not to mention extremely lucky that the virus that has gripped me for the past seven days appears, finally, to be subsiding.

Like most people, when it came to the swine flu hysteria, I was very much of the Keep Calm and Carry On school of thought. Probably won't get it, but if I do, it will be, as per the press release, "mild." I envisioned myself wrapped in a blanket, watching TCM [Turner Classic Movies] and sipping healing hot drinks. At no point did I see myself struggling with the impossible dilemma, given my body's simultaneous need for both, of whether to use the toilet in the conventional manner—or as a vomitorium.

Rapid Onset

It came on very suddenly. I had gone to bed feeling oddly thirsty, in the way that you do when you're getting a cold, and woke up with a sore throat. The headache that had been with me for about a week had intensified. I downed a couple of Neurofen, rang the office to say I would be working from home and sat down at my desk as usual. I felt bad, but OK. Just after lunch came the first bout of diarrhoea, along with a nasty sicky feeling. By teatime, as I sat watching *Dumbo* with the children, I realised that I couldn't really lift my head. Shooting pains were assailing my arms and chest, and the muscles in my legs were joining in. And I was hot, really hot. Except actually I was cold, really cold. Brrr, shivery cold. Or was I hot? I had absolutely no idea.

If I closed my eyes, I could definitely see pink elephants, though. Dancing ones, with psychedelic trombones. . . .

The next few hours are a blur. Getting my children, 6 and 4, ready for bed required every ounce of my willpower. Who knows what fabled delights I must have promised them in my delirium: trips to Disneyland, the entire Lego Star Wars collection grafted to the bedroom ceiling. It eventually worked. With the children in bed, if not actually asleep (and a bit freaked out by my uncharacteristic generosity), I decided, inexplicably, to take a very hot bath.

> ## FAST FACT
> The high fever that often accompanies flu can cause hallucinations.

It just seemed like the right thing to do. I was so unbelievably cold, and also so sweaty after my exertions: I wanted to be clean but also, crucially, warm. The relief to my aching muscles was heavenly, but it didn't last long. When my husband came home a few hours later he found me not quite asleep in his winter-weight winceyette pyjamas, clutching a hot-water bottle and shivering under two duvets and a blanket.

Husband Helps Out

Being a man of action, he brought up the laptop and logged on to the NHS [National Health Service] Swine Flu symptom-checker. I had every one of them. He took my temperature, using our superfast digital thermometer, and it was 39.8 degrees [Celsius, 103.6°F]. The next morning, after a night that is probably best left to the imagination, he called NHS Direct. The recorded message told him to phone our local surgery, which he did. The receptionist was distinctly put out. "We've very busy, you know," she said. He pressed his point. "All right, I'll see if the doctor can call you," she said, and that was that.

Around me, the day got under way. My daughter was still at school, so my husband took her on the way to the office, while my son stayed at home with our au pair [nanny]. Luckily, as both my husband and I work full time, we have childcare during the week, and so I was able to stay in bed. Goodness only knows how I would have coped if I'd have had to look after my son myself—I'm really not sure that I would have been able to. I was having trouble making it to the bathroom, let alone meeting the vigorous demands of a bumptious four-year-old boy. And at least my children are at a relatively self-sufficient age. Trying to cope with something like this with a toddler or a baby would be quite frightening, not to say dangerous.

Eventually, around 1 PM, the doctor called. She sounded harried, poor woman. It had been a nightmare morning. Anyway: what were my symptoms? By now I was finding it quite hard to speak, both because of exhaustion but mainly because my throat was so painful. Nevertheless, I managed an outline. "Oh dear, it really does sound like you have got this flu," she said. "It's hard to tell sometimes, but the chest pains are a bit of a giveaway. Do you think you want Tamiflu?" I asked her what she thought. She said that she wasn't entirely convinced, that it helped some people but that it made quite a lot of her other patients very sick. Then again, if it could help shorten the illness . . . I decided to try it.

My au pair, now promoted to "flu friend", collected the prescription and I took my first Tamiflu at around 6 PM. After about an hour, I became dimly aware of a strange foreboding in my stomach. I turned over, willing it to subside. Nope, there it was again: unmistakable. I adjusted my pillows, hoping for a reprieve. No, I was going to be sick. Really sick. I barely made it to the bathroom before my body unceremoniously ejected the Tamiflu, along with the only other thing I had swallowed that day, Ribena [a fruit drink].

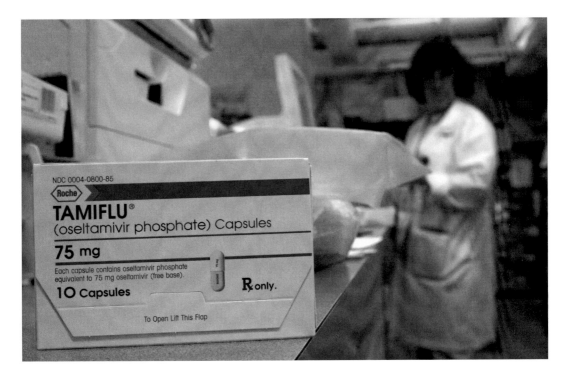

Three clean pairs of pyjamas, several packets of antibacterial wipes, a bucket of bleach and a washing machine load of unspeakably soiled linen later, my system seemed finally satisfied that the chemicals were now gone and it settled back into a straightforward fever. I couldn't face another run-in with the Tamiflu, so the night passed relatively uneventfully between dizzying trips to the bathroom and sweat-soaked sheets.

Many people with influenza, such as the author, have gotten sicker when taking Tamiflu for their symptoms. (JB Reed/ Landov)

The Misery Continues

On day three, I woke at 6 AM with only one thing in mind: antibiotics. My tonsils were so swollen that I couldn't open my mouth more than half an inch. Yesterday it was announced that a six-year-old girl who died after becoming infected with swine flu suffered septic shock as a result of tonsillitis—and Dr Mark Porter, the *Times* doctor, said that there was evidence that influenza A infection such as swine flu could increase a person's susceptibility to other infections. Having suffered from tonsillitis since I was a child, it's likely that my flu increased my susceptibility. I knew there was one cure: penicillin.

Again, my husband rang the surgery and the doctor called back. "Mm've gnot tnonsllitis," I said, sounding like I was trying to swallow a large dumpling. "Plnease gnan I hnave . . ." "Don't say another word," she said, "I can't bear it. Send your au pair, I'll give her a 'script'." She paused. "And the Tamiflu?" "Tnen tnimes wnorse," I mumbled. "Ah," she said, "So sorry. Everyone thinks that it's this big Holy Grail and it's not. Sadly, though, it's all we've got."

A Doctor Comes Down with Swine Flu

Larry Brilliant

The flu does not discriminate among the people it infects. In the following selection a man who studies epidemics becomes the victim of one. Having lived through it, Larry Brilliant expresses amazement that so many people make light of the swine flu. Although some people have termed the swine flu epidemic mild, he found it rough going. He suffered complete debilitation for three days and missed a week of work after that. If he had the opportunity, he says, he would get vaccinated against the swine flu without hesitation. Larry Brilliant is a physician and epidemiologist who took part in the successful international campaign to eradicate smallpox.

Some worry nonstop about it. Others are in denial. Many simply don't know what to think. Even more joke about it and don't give it the respect it deserves. Swine flu is the Rodney Dangerfield[1] of pandemics.

1. Deceased comedian Rodney Dangerfield's trademark comment was "I don't get no respect."

SOURCE: Larry Brilliant, "Love in the Time of Swine Flu: A Story in Three Acts," *Huffington Post*, September 22, 2009. Reprinted by permission.

There is something diminutive about the swine flu "meme" or "brand" which leads otherwise sane people to consider dismissing it, resisting vaccination whenever it becomes available. My colleagues call it a "mild pandemic"—an ironic oxymoron like "jumbo shrimp." In ten years as a professor of epidemiology,[2] I never saw the word "mild" and "pandemic" in the same paragraph, let alone used in the way the adjective "mild" seems to take the fearsome edge off of the show-stopping noun "pandemic."

We don't even agree on its name. Pork industry lobbyists pressured the mighty U.S. Government to cease calling it "swine flu" so now government agencies call it by the more readily dismissed "Novel H1N1 Influenza." Bird flu is still bird flu. Mad cow is still mad cow. Monkeypox is still monkeypox. I guess the monkey, bird, and cow lobbies weren't as effective as pork, because they are still named after their primary animal hosts, while swine flu has been unceremoniously dismounted off its first ride like a neophyte equestrian. And those in the media who have not caved in to the pork lobby can't decide whether to hyphenate it (swine-flu), capitalize it (Swine Flu), or concatenate it (swineflu). . . .

No Joking Matter

Let me tell you about my own "dance" with swine flu. . . .

"Epidemiologist gets swine flu" is not as catchy a news headline as "man bites dog" but it is cut from the same ironic cloth. And if the pandemic peaks before sufficient vaccine is available, it won't be news anymore: Just based on random probability one third to one half of doctors, epidemiologists, senators, congressmen, Heads of State, football players and Fortune 500 CEOs, cops and robbers, plumbers and celebrities will also get swine flu. And while few will die, some will, and even more will go to the ER [emergency room], or their doctor, and overwhelm

2. Epidemiology is a branch of medical science that studies the incidence, distribution, and control of disease in a population.

a health care system which is broken and does not have sufficient "surge capacity" to handle a load like this. And this pattern, plus or minus a few months, plus or minus hospital capacity, respirators, and good clinical care, will occur all over the world.

I got sick a couple of days after I had agreed to write this post for *Huffington Post,* about two weeks ago [in September 2009]. I do hope those two events were unrelated, needless to say.

Nothing Mild About It

You should not read too much into my own personal experience with the swine; yours will be different. But my swine flu was not a lovable affair, it was not a joke, and it

Health care workers receive the swine flu vaccine. Epidemiologist and viewpoint author Larry Brilliant did not receive a vaccination—a decision he would later regret when he became infected with a formidable case of swine flu. (**AP Images/ Darron Cummings**)

was not "mild." I spent three nights of aches and pains, and chills and fever. My sheets were soaked with sweat and the sound of my teeth chattering kept me awake. I tried a hot bath in the middle of the night and was so weak I could hardly get out of [the] tub unassisted. Although my temperature stayed below 102 degrees F, the teeth-chattering chills felt more like the two cases of malaria I had years ago in Asia than ordinary flu. I self-quarantined at home, drank lots of teas and sugar-free sports drinks to rehydrate, took *ibuprofen* for aches and fever and treated myself with the anti-viral drug *oseltamivir phosphate* (Tamiflu) and watched many, er, ah . . . therapeutic movies and was still out of work for a week, and weak for days afterward. But while I was never sick enough to consider going to see my doctor or going to an ER [emergency room], I would not wish this disease on anyone and I certainly would have preferred a vaccination to this teeth-rattling bug. Most poignantly, even though I tried to stay isolated, I infected one of my children who also spent a lousy sweat soaked teeth chattering week dancing with the swine. No loving parent would ever want to spread this disease to his or her kids. If the sole reason to get vaccinated were to prevent my spreading this disease to my family and community, that alone would make getting vaccinated an easy choice for me.

FAST FACT

By November 2009 the H1N1 swine flu epidemic had spread to more than two hundred countries, according to the World Health Organization.

Flu Hits Youth Hard

Bryan

Seasonal flu usually affects the elderly and very young most severely, but H1N1, also known as swine flu, is different. It seems to hit young adults and pregnant women hardest. In the following selection a college student known only as "Bryan" tells what occurred when swine flu came to his college campus. First, a friend of his came down with the flu, then Bryan awoke with it. Although he wanted to attend the football opener that weekend, he had no choice but to stay in bed. After recovering, he found that he had spread it to three of his friends. When he wrote this essay, Bryan was a marketing major at the University of Kansas.

H1N1, Swine Flu, whatever you want to call it, the virus is sweeping colleges nationwide, and some are starting to consider it a worse epidemic than Senioritis. On campus, where very little is read outside of a text message, most awareness has spread through rumors and misconceptions about the highly contagious

SOURCE: Bryan, "The Story Behind the Stats: A First Hand Account of H1N1 on Campus," October 1, 2009. www.ypulse.com. Reprinted by permission.

strand of influenza running rampant online and through classrooms and dormitories.

Like most rumors, they weren't taken seriously until some truth came from them. I personally didn't know much about H1N1, and didn't realize how serious it was in Lawrence, KS, until a friend of mine was infected. He seemed fine, and then within 24 hours of the first sign of symptoms he was MIA [missing in action]. I was only around him for about 5 minutes, and as a fairly hygienic person, figured I had little to worry about. When I first got sniffles, I laughed about it and made jokes that I should avoid eating bacon for a few days, blaming it on a bad day of allergies.

The Flu Hits

But the joke was on me when I woke the next morning with a laundry-list of flu-like symptoms and even less desire than usual to get out of bed. I went to the health center, where I found many of my peers in the same state of sickness as myself. I realized, at age 20, I was no longer an invincible teenager and had succumbed to the dreaded H1N1 virus. My initially nonchalant reaction turned into fear as I considered the amount of hospitalizations and deaths associated with it and, trust me, when you are feeling like death, the paranoia gets amplified.

I began to do some research and discovered the University of Kansas (my school) was featured on CNN with over 300 cases reported. I was officially a statistic, and the latest rumor circulating was that the number may be as much as 10 times greater, as many cases go unreported. Luckily I started feeling sick on a Thursday, so I spent the weekend resting. Unluckily it was the same weekend as the home-opener for football, so it was more of a challenge to stay in bed than one would imagine.

FAST FACT

According to National Public Radio, during the first week of classes in the fall of 2009, more than sixteen hundred cases of swine flu were reported on US college campuses.

A few of my infected friends did not resist the temptation to tailgate and tried to apply some home remedies towards eliminating the virus. These attempts, from my observations, were not successful.

Classroom Confusion

The widespread chaos caused by the virus infected academic life as well. Teachers were not prepared for the waves of absences which occurred; many of which were caused by a single student not willing to miss a lecture and infecting everyone in the classroom. The result was a large amount of confusion, and at least one student's prediction that many GPAs will fall below average compared to past years due to the week-long recovery time needed to return to full strength. At the University of Florida, another student, Liz, shared similar concerns, but says professors are slightly better prepared to deal with the academic-pandemic as classes are able to be watched online.

Although some students have seen print campaigns on campus regarding swine flu, most information they interpret only results in misunderstandings. Many people who report flu-like symptoms do not believe they have H1N1 as they feel that swine is a very severe strand of the flu and milder symptoms indicate a different strand. The biggest difference most notice is how contagious their sickness seems to be compared with past flu seasons. After showing first symptoms, within 72 hours I had spread it to my 3 roommates, and quite a few friends. It seems the only defense is luck, as even an exceptional immune system and extra doses of Vitamin C proved ineffective.

GLOSSARY

adjuvant A substance added to a vaccine to boost the immune response it evokes in the body.

antibiotic A medicine that kills or disables bacteria; not effective against viruses.

antibody A destructive protein produced by the body's immune system in response to a foreign substance that the immune system recognizes as a danger.

antigen Any foreign substance that stimulates the body's immune system to produce antibodies.

antiviral A medicine that works to disable or disrupt viruses that cause disease.

avian flu A highly contagious and often deadly influenza that mainly attacks birds but sometimes infects humans.

epidemic An outbreak of disease that sweeps through a population in a certain geographically defined area, such as a region or country

H5N1 A type of avian influenza that is especially deadly. It has been known to spread from fowls to people through direct contact, but not to jump from person to person.

H1N1 A type of flu virus that originally infected swine but soon spread to people. The H stands for hemagglutinin, the N for neuraminidase.

hemagglutinin A spike-shaped protein that extends from the surface of a flu virus. It binds to specific sugar chains on cellular proteins and allows the virus to break into the cell.

host An organism that an infectious agent occupies. *See* infections agent.

immune system The body's cells, tissues, and organs that help fight off infection.

infectious agent Any organism, such as a pathogenic virus, parasite, or bacterium, that is capable of invading a body, causing disease, and spreading to another body.

influenza An infectious viral disease characterized by inflammation and congestion of the respiratory tract, high fever, muscle aches, chills, and in extreme cases, death.

mutation An alteration in a gene from its original state. Mutation contributes to evolution.

neuraminidase A surface protein on the influenza virus that acts as an essential enzyme in the spread of the virus from inside an infected cell.

pandemic The worldwide outbreak of a disease.

pathogen An agent such as a virus or bacterium capable of causing a disease.

quarantine The enforced isolation of an infected person or animal to prevent the spread of disease.

seasonal flu An annually recurrent type of flu that typically flares up in winter.

strain A distinctive set of organisms within a species or variety.

vaccine A protective substance that contains deactivated pathogens or components of a pathogen intended to stimulate an immune response. Once vaccinated, a person is usually able to fight off an infection from a similar pathogen.

virulent Capable of causing severe illness or death.

virus   An assembly of genetic materials within a protein coat that, while not capable of independent life or replication, is able to infect and hijack cells to reproduce itself.

World Health Organization   The World Health Organization, an agency of the United Nations that integrates and coordinates the public health efforts of member nations.

CHRONOLOGY

B.C. 412 Greek physician Hippocrates describes a disease that may have been the flu.

ca. 200 The Charaka Samhita, an ancient Ayurvedic text from India, refers to a disease that appears to be the flu. It recommends hot water and a change of diet as treatment.

A.D. 1357 The term *influenza* is coined. It comes from the Italian word meaning "influence," a reference to the supposed effect of the stars on the development of flu.

1485 A flu-like "sweating disease" sweeps through Britain, leaving many dead.

1580 The first influenza pandemic on record starts in Europe and makes its way to Asia and Africa.

1803 A harsh flu season prompts the publication of a satirical print in London titled "An Address of Thanks from the Faculty to the Right Honble. (Honorable) Mr. Influenzy for his kind visit to this country."

1889 The Russian flu sweeps across Western Europe, crosses the English Channel, and hits the United Kingdom. Its unusually high mortality rate stirs fear and rumor.

1918–1919 Following World War I, the Spanish flu rapidly spreads around the world, killing millions—especially young people. It is the worst pandemic in modern times.

ca. 1928   Researcher Richard Shope shows that swine flu can be transmitted through filtered mucus, implying that influenza is caused by a virus, since nothing larger could get through.

1933   Researchers Christopher Andrewes, Wilson Smith, and Patrick Laidlaw isolate a human influenza virus.

1940   Frank Macfarlane Burnet grows flu viruses in a lab using chicken eggs.

1957   A relatively mild flu pandemic makes its way across the globe.

1968–1969   The Hong Kong flu causes a flu pandemic. Though frightening, it leads to relatively few deaths.

circa 1975   The role of migratory birds in circulating influenza virus is discovered.

1976   Swine flu breaks out among soldiers stationed at Fort Dix, New Jersey. One dies, and a major panic follows. The administration of President Gerald Ford orders a massive vaccination campaign that ends up causing more harm than the flu it was intended to stop.

1983   A massive outbreak of bird flu strikes the US poultry industry, leading to the deaths of 17 million farm birds.

1997   The first known human case of the avian flu, known as H5N1, ends in the death of the patient in Hong Kong. Other deaths follow in Asia and the Middle East.

2009   A new strain of swine flu, called H1N1, breaks out in Mexico. As it rapidly spreads, the World Health Organization declares a pandemic, and massive efforts to vaccinate people get under way.

2010   As the H1N1 pandemic subsides, epidemiologists realize that its effect, in the United States at least, has been milder than the seasonal flu. Nevertheless, it causes some tragic deaths, especially among pregnant women.

ORGANIZATIONS TO CONTACT

The editors have compiled the following list of organizations concerned with the issues debated in this book. The descriptions are derived from materials provided by the organizations. All have publications or information available for interested readers. The list was compiled on the date of publication of the present volume; the information provided here may change. Be aware that many organizations take several weeks or longer to respond to inquiries, so allow as much time as possible.

American Society for Microbiology
1752 N St. NW
Washington, DC
20036-2904
(202) 737-3600
fax: (202) 942-9333
e-mail: oed@asmusa
.org
website: www.asm.org

The American Society for Microbiology is the oldest and largest member-based life science organization in the world. It works to improve microbiological sciences as a way to respond to infectious diseases. Among its goals are to support programs of education, training, and public information and to advance knowledge through journals, books, meetings, and workshops.

Centers for Disease Control and Prevention (CDC)
1600 Clifton Rd.
Atlanta, GA 30333
(800) CDC-INFO
fax: (770) 488-4760
e-mail: cdcinfo@cdc
.gov
website: www.cdc.gov

The CDC is the nation's leading agency to prevent and control infectious diseases. Based in Atlanta, Georgia, the CDC works with public health departments, hospitals, and health care providers across the nation to track outbreaks of infectious diseases such as influenza and recommends action to contain or prevent their spread.

Infectious Diseases Society of America (IDSA)
1300 Wilson Blvd.
Ste. 300
Arlington, VA 22209
(703) 299-0200
fax: (703) 299-0204
website: www.id society.org

The IDSA is a nonprofit organization representing physicians, scientists, and other health care professionals who specialize in infectious diseases. Its purpose is to improve the health of individuals, communities, and society by promoting excellence in patient care, education, research, public health, and prevention relating to infectious diseases.

International Society for Infectious Diseases (ISID)
9 Babcock St., Unit 3
Brookline, MA 02446
(617) 277-0551
fax: (617) 278-9113
e-mail: info@isid.org
website: www.isid.org

The ISID is committed to improving the care of patients with infectious diseases, the training of clinicians and researchers in infectious diseases and microbiology, and the control of infectious diseases around the world. The society recognizes that infectious diseases cross all national and regional boundaries and that effective long-term solutions require international scientific exchange and cooperation. ISID and its members are dedicated to developing partnerships and to finding solutions to the problem of infectious diseases across the globe.

Mayo Clinic
200 First St. SW
Rochester, MN 55905
(507) 284-2511
fax: (507) 284-0161
website: www.mayo clinic.org

The Mayo Clinic, based in Rochester, Minnesota, is a not-for-profit medical center that diagnoses and treats complex medical problems in every specialty, including infectious diseases such as influenza. The clinic maintains a public website with links to more than six hundred articles and entries on virtually every type of disease.

National Center for Emerging and Zoonotic Infectious Diseases (NCEZID)
Centers for Disease Control and Prevention
1600 Clifton Rd.
Atlanta, GA 30333
(800) 232-4636
e-mail: cdcinfo@cdc
.gov
website: www.cdc.gov
/ncezid

The NCEZID, a unit of the CDC, aims to prevent disease, disability, and death caused by a wide range of infectious diseases. It focuses on old and new diseases, as well as zoonotic diseases, which are those spread from animals to people.

National Foundation for Infectious Diseases (NFID)
4733 Bethesda Ave.
Ste. 750
Bethesda, MD 20814
(301) 656-0003
fax: (301) 907-0878
e-mail: info@nfid.org
website: www.nfid.org

The NFID is a nonprofit organization founded in 1973. It is dedicated to educating the public and health care professionals about the causes, treatment, and prevention of infectious diseases. The NFID carries out its mission by educating health care professionals and the public and by supporting research.

National Institute of Allergy and Infectious Diseases (NIAID)
6610 Rockledge Dr.
MSC 6612
Bethesda, MD 20892-6612T
(866) 284-4107
fax: (301) 402-3573
e-mail: ocpostoffice@
niaid.nih.gov
website: www.niaid
.nih.gov

The NIAID conducts and supports basic and applied research to better understand, treat, and ultimately prevent infectious, immunologic, and allergic diseases. For more than sixty years, NIAID research has led to new therapies, vaccines, diagnostic tests, and other technologies that have improved the health of millions of people in the United States and around the world.

Vaccine and Infectious Disease Organization (VIDO-InterVac)
120 Veterinary Rd.
Saskatoon, SK, S7N 5E3 Canada
(306) 966-7465
fax: (306) 966-7478
e-mail: vido.communications@usask.ca
website: www.vido.org

VIDO-InterVac is a research institute located on the campus of the University of Saskatchewan in Saskatoon, Saskatchewan, Canada. With support from the Canadian government, it carries out research into the pathogenesis of infectious diseases and the development of effective therapeutic and protective methods to control infectious diseases that attack humans and animals.

World Health Organization (WHO)
20 Avenue Appia
1211 Geneva 27
Switzerland
+ 41 22 791 21 11
fax: + 41 22 791 31 11
e-mail: info@who.int
website: www.who.int

The WHO is the main authority for health matters within the United Nations system. It is responsible for providing leadership on global health matters, shaping the health research agenda, setting norms and standards, articulating evidence-based policy options, providing technical support to countries, and monitoring and assessing health trends. It plays a central role in tracking influenza around the world.

FOR FURTHER READING

Books

Larry Altshuler, *The Bird-Flu Primer*. New York: Sterling & Ross, 2006.

Alfred Crosby, *America's Forgotten Pandemic: The Influenza of 1918*. New York: Cambridge University Press, 1989.

Pete Davies, *The Devil's Flu*. New York: Henry Holt, 2000.

Mike Davis, *The Monster at Our Door: The Global Threat of Avian Flu*. New York: New Press, 2005.

Jeffrey Greene with Karen Moline, *The Bird Flu Pandemic: Can It Happen? Will It Happen?* New York: Thomas Dunne, 2006.

Gina Kolata, *Flu: The Story of the Great Influenza Pandemic of 1918 and the Search for the Virus That Caused It*. New York: Touchstone, 1999.

Michael Markopoulos, *Swine Flu, 2010 Edition: The Survivor's Guide*. Del Mar, CA: Michael Markopoulos, M.D., 2009.

Terence Stephenson, *Swine Flu H1N1: The Facts*. London: Jessica Kingsley, 2009.

Periodicals and Internet Sources

Tim Appenzeller, "Tracking the Next Killer Flu," *National Geographic*, October 2005.

Mary Carmichael, "Swine Flu and Pregnancy: What Your Doctor Might Not Tell You," *Newsweek*, September 29, 2009.

Jon Cohen, "Scientists Ponder Swine Flu's Origins," *Science*, May 8, 2009.

Christophe Fraser et al. "Pandemic Potential of a Strain of Influenza A (H1N1): Early Findings," *Science*, June 19, 2009.

Serena Gordon, "Mom's Flu Shot May Protect Baby After Birth," HealthDay, October 5, 2010. http://consumer.healthday.com/Article.asp?AID=643935.

Amina Khan, "Popular Kids Get Flu First; That's Good News for the Wallflowers, Researchers Say," *Los Angeles Times*, September 16, 2010.

Inga Kiderra, "The Friendly Way to Catch the Flu," National Science Foundation, September 20, 2010. http://www.usnews .com/science/articles/2010/09/20/the-friendly-way-to-catch-the-flu.html.

Debora MacKenzie, "Tests Dash Hopes of Rapid Production of Bird Flu Vaccine," *New Scientist*, December 16, 2005.

Meredith Melnick, "American Academy of Pediatrics: Make the Flu Shot Mandatory," *Time*, September 8, 2010.

Morbidity & Mortality Weekly Report, "2009 Pandemic Influenza A (H1N1) in Pregnant Women Requiring Intensive Care— New York City," March 26, 2010. www.cdc.gov/mmwr/preview /mmwrhtml/mm5911a1.htm.

Alice Park, "Post-H1N1, Why You Still Need to Worry About Flu," *Time*, September 12, 2010.

Robert Preidt, "H1N1 Protection in Coming Season's Flu Vaccines: FDA," HealthDay, July 30, 2010. www.nlm.nih.gov/med lineplus/news/fullstory_101687.html.

Janet Raloff, "Dry Air Might Boost Flu Transmission," *Science News*, September 15, 2010.

Shari Roan, "Flu Vaccine in Pregnancy Curbs Infant Illness," *Los Angeles Times*, October 4, 2010.

Bret Stephens, "Swine-Flu Hysteria," *Wall Street Journal*, May 5, 2009.

Terrence M. Tumpey, "Characterization of the Reconstructed 1918 Spanish Influenza Pandemic Virus," *Science*, October 14, 2005.

Andreas von Bubnoff, "The 1918 Virus Is Resurrected," *Nature*, September 22, 2005.

Robert G. Webster, "The Importance of Animal Influenza for Human Disease," *Vaccine*, no. 20, 2002.

INDEX

A

Additives, in vaccines, 93
Advisory Committee on Immunization
   Practices (ACIP), 88
Antiviral drugs, 21, 66
Asian flu pandemic (1957–1958), 16, 77
Avian (H5N1) influenza, 25
   confirmed human cases of, 62–66
   deaths from, in Asia/Middle East, *61*
   is threat to human life, 59–67
   symptoms/treatment of, 66
   viral subtypes of, 60

B

Barbosa, Jarbus, 80
Barrett, Julia, 15
Bioterrorism, 18, 43
Blaser, Martin, 78
Brillant, Larry, 101

C

Califano, Joseph, 39
Campylobacter, 84
CDC. *See* Centers for Disease Control
   and Prevention
Celvapan, 85–86
Centers for Disease Control and
   Prevention (CDC), 59, 84
   advisory board on vaccine
      recommendations, 88
   on deaths from influenza, 10, 78
   H1N1-positive tests reported to, *27*
Clinical Infectious Diseases (journal), 75

D

Deaths/death rates
   from avian flu in Asia/Middle East, *61*
   in flu pandemics, 77
   from Guillain-Barré syndrome related to
      swine flu vaccination, 38
   in H1N1 flu pandemic, 71, 70, *72*, 78, 80
   from influenza *vs.* other causes, 80
   from seasonal flu, *19, 42*
   in Spanish flu pandemic, 31, *32*
Derlet, Robert, 41
Direct immunofluorescence antibody
   (DFA) staining, 43
DNA (deoxyribonucleic acid), 10
Duncan, Arne, 70

E

Eckstrand, Irene, 57–58
Elderly
   flu vaccine and development of
      pneumonia in, 89–91
   influenza deaths among, 17
   response to influenza vaccine among, 50

F

Fauci, Anthony S., 51–52
FDA (Food and Drug Administration,
   US), 50
FluID$_X$ diagnostic system, 41, 43–45, *44*
Food and Drug Administration, US
   (FDA), 50
Ford, Gerald, 11, 37
Frey, Rebecca J., 15